What Everyone Needs To Know About THE BIBLE

By
Don Stewart

What Everyone Needs To Know About THE BIBLE

By
Don Stewart

What Everyone Needs To Know About The Bible

Published by Dart Press
Box 6486
Orange, California 92613

ISBN 1-877825-08-5

PRINTED IN THE UNITED STATES OF AMERICA BY
GILLILAND PRINTING INC.
215 NORTH SUMMIT
ARKANSAS CITY, KANSAS 67005

All Scripture quotations are from the New King James Version unless otherwise noted.

Contents

Introductory Topics

Historical Accuracy

Inspiration And Authority

52. Why Are The Writings Of The Apostle Paul Considered To Be Inspired?

53. To What Extent Is The Bible Inspired?

54. What Is Inerrancy?

55. Does The Bible Testify To Its Own Inerrancy?

56. Has The Church Historically Taught That The Bible Is Inerrant?

57. Is The Doctrine Of Inerrancy Important?

58. Does Inerrancy Extend To All Matters Scientific And Historical?

59. What Objections Have Been Made Against Inerrancy?

60. Did Jesus Believe The Scriptures Were Without Error?

Canon

61. What Is The Canon Of Scripture?

62. Who Decided Which Books Should Be Placed In The Bible?

63. What Criteria Were Used In Determining Which Books Belonged In The Bible?

64. How Do We Know The Correct Books Are In The Bible?

65. Do Jews And Christians Use The Same Old Testament?

66. What Effect Did The Council of Nicea Have In Determining What Books Belonged in The Bible?

67. Should Other Early Writings Be Placed In The Bible?

68. Why Was The Authority Of Certain Old Testament Books Questioned?

Interpretation And Application

Introduction

The Bible is the world's number one best seller. No other book even comes close. Why? Why has this one books sold so many millions of copies throughout its history? What makes the Bible so special?

The purpose of this present volume is to answer some of the most often asked questions about the Bible. The questions are addressed so that the reader may formulate his or her own opinion about what type of book the Bible is. We will explore such subjects as the nature of the Bible, its historical reliability, and its application to daily life.

The book is divided into six sections. They are as follows:

Introductory Topics

The first section answers questions concerning introductory matters about the Bible such as: What is it? To whom was it written? What impact has the Bible on humanity?

Textual Criticism

The second section deals with the text of the Old and New Testaments. These questions include: Is the text reliable? Has the text of the Bible been changed as it has been copied and recopied throughout history? How do we know what it originally said?

Historical Accuracy

In the third section we will answer questions concerning the historical accuracy of Scripture: Is the history recorded in the pages of Scripture accurate? Should we trust the historical portrait the Bible gives about Jesus?

Inspiration and Authority

We then come to questions dealing with the inspiration and authority of Scripture, such as: What do we mean when we speak of revelation? What is inspiration? How has God revealed Himself to mankind? To what extent is the Bible inspired?

Canon

The subject of canon (authoritative books) is dealt with next: Are there books in Scripture that do not belong? Are there other writings that should be added to the Bible?

Interpretation and Application

The last section deal with issues of interpretation and application. These include: How is the Bible supposed to be interpreted? How can a person apply the teaching of the Bible to his daily life? How can a person know the Bible is God's Word?

Test its Claims

The Apostle Paul wrote,

> Test all things; hold fast what is good (1 Thessalonians 5:21).

We invite the reader to test the claims of Scripture to see if it is what it claims to be—the Word of God.

PART 1

INTRODUCTORY TOPICS

WHAT IS THE BIBLE?

Our English word Bible means "book." It is derived from the Latin word *biblia* and the Greek *biblos*. From the second century A.D. the Christian church has used the term *Bible* to refer to the sixty-six books that they hold to be sacred Scripture.

The Bible is made up of two testaments, the Old and the New. There are thirty-nine books in the Old Testament and twenty-seven in the New Testament. The Old Testament was composed from about 1400 to 400 B.C., while the New Testament was written from approximately A.D. 50 to A.D. 90.

God's Word

The Bible claims to be the Word of God, that is, His communication to humanity. Over three thousand times in the Old Testament alone we find such phrases as, "Thus says the Lord," or "God said." For centuries people have turned to the Bible for the answers to the basic questions of life: Where did we come from? Why are we here on Planet Earth? What will happen to us when we die?

Nature of God

The Bible tells us about the character of God. Within its pages we find a personal infinite God who created the entire universe—and created man in His image.

Purpose for History

The Bible also gives a purpose for history. History is not merely a series of unrelated events, as the Bible records it; history has meaning. The Bible shows a progression to an end, and promises that the world in which we live, with all its corruption, will one day be made into a new world without sin.

Basis for Science

Though this may surprise some, the Bible served as a basis for modern scientific pursuits. Modern science was born in the seventeenth century because of a belief in an unchanging God or order, purpose and consistency—the God portrayed in the Bible.

Law and Order

Our modern concept of law and order are also based on the Bible. The Bible says that God has set standards of right and wrong behavior. Many of our current laws are based upon Biblical morality.

Daily Needs

Finally, millions of Christians have depended on the Bible's promises that God would meet their daily needs. The Apostle Paul wrote,

> And my God shall supply all your need according to His riches in glory by Christ Jesus (Philippians 4:19).

The Book of Hebrews assures the believer,

> For He Himself has said, 'I will never leave you nor forsake you' (Hebrews 13:5).

Thus the Bible is not just a building block of our society, but is a practical help to countless individuals.

One Book

The Bible, though consisting of sixty-six books, is actually one book. It claims to be God's Word to humanity. The Bible offers answers to life's basic questions. These include the existence and nature of God, the identity and purpose of man, the meaning of history, and scientific questions about the nature of the universe. The Bible also provides a basis of right and wrong as well as a practical guide for daily needs.

Whether or not we accept its claims, we must recognize its importance. Throughout the centuries, the Bible has wielded great influence. We could reasonably call it the most important book in the world. It is of the utmost importance, therefore, that we understand its makeup, contents and claims.

IS THE BIBLE GOD'S WORD?

The Bible claims to be God's communication to humanity; but is that claim true? How can we test it out?

Arguing in a Circle?

Many opponents of Christianity complain that Christians try to prove the Bible by quoting the Bible. They are thus reasoning in a circle and still begging the question of the Bible's reliability. There is some validity to this complaint. Although it is important to understand what the Bible says in order to test its internal consistency, it is also possible to establish the Bible's authority on independent grounds.

Some Christians believe the only way to know for sure that the Bible is the true Word of God is to try it out, to believe it, to trust it. Once a person is inside God's truth, they say, the reliability of it becomes apparent. This has been true for many people, but it overlooks the fact that the Bible stands up to objective scrutiny. We can investigate the Bible from the inside or from the outside, and we find it to be true, if we honestly evaluate the evidence.

This book presents some of the evidence. At the center of the investigation is Jesus. Jesus claimed to be the unique Son of God, God in human flesh. And He backed up His claim with the most remarkable event in history, He came back from the dead, as He said He would. We can reasonably accept His resurrection as a historical fact not only because of the multi-faceted testimony of the early Christians, which was collected in the New Testament, but because no one has successfully disproved it. Christianity had many enemies in its first few decades—enemies who would have been thrilled to show the errors of Christianity, if they could. The would have rushed to dig up Jesus' body and thoroughly debunk the resurrection, but they could not because He had risen.

Christianity Makes Sense

It is thus reasonable to believe that Jesus was whom He said He was. In that case, we would expect His followers to collect His public and private sayings and deeds and record them faithfully—which is exactly what the Gospels claim to be.

In the Gospels, we find that Jesus not only accepted but advanced the Jews' idea that God had spoken to them in their Scriptures. Thus Jesus Himself affirmed the divine origin of the Old Testament. He also promised that God's Spirit would help His followers remember His own words and works. So it makes sense that God would inspire the New Testament as He had the Old Testament. Jesus repeatedly taught that the Hebrew Scriptures prophesied about Him. Certainly God would take as much care in communicating the fulfillment of those prophecies as He had in the prophecies themselves.

The Bible's claim to be the Word of God is a reasonable conclusion drawn from the evidence. Throughout the remainder of this book we will present some of that evidence and also deal with some of the common challenges to the Bible's authority.

WHY IS THE BIBLE NECESSARY?

The Bible says that human beings are not able to understand God through their own reasoning powers, because:

Communication Has Been Broken

When Adam and Eve disobeyed God's commandment, the communication between them and God was severed. God had warned them of the result:

> But of the tree of the knowledge of good and evil you shall not eat, for in the day that you eat of it you shall surely die (Genesis 2:17).

The main idea behind death is separation. When Adam and Eve disobeyed God, they suffered a spiritual separation from God. Before that time, man had direct access to God. This is no longer true.

God is Unapproachable

God, by His very nature, cannot be approached by sinful man. The Apostle Paul described God in this way:

> Who alone has immortality, dwelling in unapproachable light, whom no man has seen or can see (1 Timothy 6:16).

Thus, by His very nature God is separated from man.

Natural Man

The Bible designates our sinful condition by calling us "natural man." The natural man, blinded by sin, cannot know God through his own wisdom.

> But the natural man does not receive the things of the Spirit of God, for they are foolishness to him; nor can he know them for they are spiritually discerned (1 Corinthians 2:14).

Because of these factors—the broken communication between God and man, the inaccessibility of God, and the fact that sinful man cannot know the things of God—a revelation from God is absolutely essential.

No Hope Without It

Without God's divine revelation in the Bible, we are left to our own ideas about who God is and who we are. Any attempt to explain God is doomed to failure because each of us would merely project our own thoughts about who God is and come up with the type of God we think should exist. There would be no consensus of opinion and no basis of knowing who, if anybody, is right in his opinions about God. With God's divine revelation as it is written in the Bible, there is no confusion surrounding God's character.

IS IT LOGICAL TO THINK THAT GOD COMMUNICATES TO US?

Some people have ruled out the possibility of God communicating with humanity. They believe a revelation from a divine being to man is not possible. However, the idea that God would communicate to humanity and leave a written Word make sense for the following reasons:

Personal God

The Bible reveals that the God who exists is a personal God; that is, He has the characteristics of personhood. He thinks, feels, and can give and receive love. He also has the ability to communicate. The Bible says that God loves His people.

We Can Communicate

God made man in His image and likeness. Part of that likeness is the ability to give and receive communication. Since both God and man have the ability to communicate, it is perfectly logical to assume that He would communicate with us.

We Have A Communication

With these factors considered, a final point to emphasize is that we do, in fact, have a written communication that claims to be from God. That communication, the Bible shows us a God who loves to reveal Himself. The prophet Isaiah said:

> Hear O heavens, and give ear O earth! For the Lord has spoken (Isaiah 1:2).

Simon Peter said to Jesus,

> Lord, to whom shall we go? You have the words of eternal life (John 6:68).

God is a Communicator

There is no doubt that the Bible presents a consistent portrait of God as a communicator. The Bible itself is His major communication.

This may look like circular reasoning to some: the Bible proving itself. But that's not really the case. If we grant that the Bible has any validity at all, we have to recognize that it is filled, from cover to cover, with this sense of a communicating God. Within itself, it is consistent. If we, on the other hand, maintain that it is illogical to think that God communicates to us, then our God has little relation to the God of the Bible. Our system is closed. We are shutting out evidence that may prove valuable.

It is logical to think that God communicates with us. From a purely objective standpoint, it would be unwise to dismiss the possibility of a communicating God.

TO WHOM WAS THE BIBLE WRITTEN?

The appeal of the Bible is universal, addressed to all mankind. It is a book that everyone can understand. The Bible says that when Jesus spoke, "the common people heard Him gladly" (Mark 12:37). The multitudes listened and followed Him. Jesus encouraged the children to be brought to Him:

> Let the little children come to Me, and do not forbid them; for of such is the kingdom of heaven (Matthew 19:14).

Certain parts of the Scripture are written to individuals and specific groups, but even these have both special and universal application.

Everyday Language

One way that we know the Bible was written for everyone is the language in which it was composed. As recently as one hundred years ago, we did not possess any Greek writings that were contemporary with the New Testament. The Greek of the New Testament was different from the classical Greek of Plato and Sophocles. Most scholars speculated that it was some kind of "Holy Ghost" language. In 1863 Bishop Lightfoot, with rare insight, conjectured about the language of the New Testament. He wrote that New Testament Greek,

> . . . probably had been part of the common speech all along. I will go further, and say that if we could only recover letters that ordinary people wrote to each other without any thought of being literary, we should have the greatest possible help for the understanding of the language of the New Testament generally (cited by George Milligan, *Selections from Greek Papyri*, Chicago, Ares, 1980).

Since his time, the letters of ordinary people have been found written on pieces of pottery, papyrus, wood, and stone. His prediction was correct. It became clear that the New Testament was written in the common, everyday language of the people, not some special language. This reinforces the idea that the Bible was written to the masses, not just an elite few.

Everyone Held Responsible

The Bible claims to have universal authority over all people everywhere. There are only two categories of people according to the Bible, believers and unbelievers. The New Testament says:

> He who believes in the Son has everlasting life; and he who does not believe the Son shall not see life, but the wrath of God abides on him (John 3:36).

We conclude that the Bible was written to everyone, not just a select few.

WHAT DOES THE OLD TESTAMENT SAY ABOUT ITSELF?

We find in the Old Testament's the concept that the words and deeds it records come from the living God.

The Old Testament claims to record the words of God:

> And Aaron spoke all the words which the Lord had spoken to Moses (Exodus 4:30).

The Old Testament says the following concerning itself:

Conveyed Through Humans

> Yes, they made their hearts like flint, refusing to hear the law and the words which the Lord of hosts had sent by His Spirit through the former prophets (Zechariah 7:12).

Benefit Future Generations

The Scriptures were recorded for the benefit of future generations.

> As for Me, says the Lord, 'this is My covenant with them: My Spirit who is upon you, and My words which I have put in your mouth, shall not depart from your mouth, nor from the mouth of your descendants, nor from the mouth of your descendants' descendants . . . from this time and forevermore (Isaiah 58:21).

Infallible

> God is not a man that He should lie, nor a son of man, that He should repent. Has He said, and will He not do it? Or has He spoken and will He not make it good (Numbers 23:19).

Eternal and Unchanging

> The grass withers, the flower fades, but the word of our God stands forever (Isaiah 40:8).

> Forever, O Lord, Your word is settled in heaven (Psalm 119:89).

Powerful

> Is not My word like a fire? says the Lord, and like a hammer that breaks the rock in pieces? (Jeremiah 23:29).

True

> Your law is truth (Psalm 119:142).

Perfect

> The law of the Lord is perfect, converting the soul (Psalm 19:7).

Accomplishes its Purpose

> So shall My word be that goes forth from My mouth; it shall not return to Me void, but it shall accomplish what I please, and it shall prosper in the thing for which I sent it (Isaiah 55:11).

Guide for Daily Living

> Your word is a lamp to my feet and a light to my path (Psalm 119:105).

From these statements contained in the Old Testament, we can see that it claims to record the words and deeds of God. We also observe that the statements made about God's Word assure us that we can place our trust in His promises.

WHAT DOES THE NEW TESTAMENT SAY ABOUT ITSELF?

The New Testament, like the Old Testament, also claims to record the words of God. Paul reminded the church in Thessalonica:

> When you received the word of God which you heard from us, you welcomed it not as the word of men, but as it is in truth, the word of God (1 Thessalonians 2:13).

As was true with the Old Testament, God's Word was conveyed through human instrumentation:

> These things we also speak, not in words which man's wisdom teaches but which the Holy Spirit teaches (1 Corinthians 2:13).

The New Testament says this about itself:

Authoritative

The Word of God is presented as the final authority on all matters, as Jesus demonstrated in response to His temptation.

> Then Jesus said to him, "Away with you, Satan! For it is written, 'You shall worship the Lord your God, and Him only you shall serve' " (Matthew 4:10).

Eternal

Jesus said His words were everlasting:

> Heaven and earth will pass away, but My words will by no means pass away (Matthew 24:35).

True

Jesus also affirmed that God's Word is true in all that it says:

> Sanctify them by Your truth. Your word is truth (John 17:17).

Hence, both testaments claim to record the words and deeds of God.

WHY IS A WRITTEN RECORD FROM GOD IMPORTANT?

Is it possible that man can know God apart from a revelation that was committed to writing. There are several reasons why a written revelation is necessary.

Misinterpretation

If we were given only an oral communication from God, then we would have a message that could be changed and misinterpreted when repeatedly told. The more the story was repeated orally, the more the story could be changed. This would not give us much confidence in the message.

Moreover, if the message began to differ considerably, how would anyone know which version to trust? A revelation from God based upon oral communication would be beset with many problems.

Preservation

Once the words and deeds have been committed to writing, the message can be preserved. This allows succeeding generations to have the benefit of seeing what the original writers said. By putting the messages in a book, such as the Bible, the truth can be preserved from future generations. God continues to speak, though the original receptors of the message have died.

Authoritative Source

A written revelation solves doctrinal controversies. If there is a question of Christian belief, the written Bible can be studied as an authoritative source.

Translated

Once a revelation is committed to writing, there is a greater possibility of transmitting it to those of a different language.

Spread the Message

The message can be spread and copied with the assurance that the original thoughts will stay intact. All of these factors demonstrate the necessity of a written revelation from God.

ARE THERE OTHER WRITTEN SOURCES OF RELIGIOUS TRUTH APART FROM THE BIBLE?

The Bible clearly says that it is the sole source of our knowledge about the one true living God.

Not to Add or Subtract

There are warnings contained in Scripture not to add or subtract from what God has revealed:

> You shall not add to the word which I command you, nor take anything from it, that you may keep the commandments of the Lord your God which I command you (Deuteronomy 4:2).

> Every word of God is pure; He is a shield to those who put their trust in Him. Do not add to His words, lest He reprove you, and you be found a liar (Proverbs 30:5,6).

Other Ways False

The Bible warns its readers of false prophets and false teachings.

> Beloved, do not believe every spirit, but test the spirits, whether they are of God; because many false prophets have gone out in the world (1 John 4:1).

Jesus warned of those who offer other ways to approach God:

> I am the door of the sheep. All who ever came before Me are thieves and robbers, but the sheep did not hear them. I am the door. If anyone enters by Me, he will be saved (John 10:7-9).

It is clear, then, that the Bible does not present itself as one of several options for religious truth. It claims to be God's authoritative Word, and it maintains that any work, religious or otherwise, which teaches anything to the contrary is, at that point, wrong. As far as the Bible is concerned, it's all or nothing. If we accept it, we must accept it as ultimately authoritative. It must be the standard by which we judge all other revelations.

DOES THE BIBLE TELL US EVERYTHING WE WANT TO KNOW ABOUT GOD?

The Bible does not promise to tell us everything we *want* to know, just everything we *need* to know.

Written for a Purpose

The Bible was written for the purpose of creating belief in God. The Apostle John wrote:

> And truly Jesus did many other signs in the presence of His disciples, which are not written in this book; but these are written that you may believe that Jesus is the Christ, the Son of God, and that believing you may have life in His name (John 20:30,31).

John informs us that his book was composed for the purpose of creating belief in God through the person Jesus Christ.

True But Not Exhaustive

Yet the Bible never claims to be exhaustive. The Apostle John told his readers that he did not record all the acts of Jesus that he witnessed.

> And there are also many other things that Jesus did, which if they were written one by one, I suppose that even

> the world itself could not contain the books that would be written (John 21:25).

The Bible is the record of God acting in history. It tells us enough that we need to know concerning God, ourselves, and how we can enter into an eternal relationship with God. But it does not reveal to us every mystery of His kingdom, or recall every detail of the events therein, nor does it prophesy every future event.

Christ Alone?

Some people object to the idea of identifying the Bible with the Word of God by saying Christ alone is the Word of God. They say that it is a mistake to identify the Bible as God's Word. Yet, in the Bible, we find the term *word* refers to both Jesus Christ and the written Scripture.

Christ the Word

The Bible teaches that Jesus Christ is the Word of God:

> In the beginning was the Word, and the Word was with God and the Word was God . . . And the Word became flesh and dwelt among us (John 1:1,14).

Jesus is the living Word of God who came to earth from heaven's glory to reveal to man what God is like. The writer to the Hebrews said,

> God, who at various times and in different ways spoke in time past to the fathers by the prophets, has in these last days spoken to us by His Son (Hebrews 1:1,2).

Hence, the Bible teaches that Christ is God's Word to mankind.

Yet the only way we can know Jesus Christ, the living Word of God, is through the written Word of God, the Bible. The only true Jesus is the biblical Jesus and the only authoritative work that reveals the true Jesus is the Bible.

We conclude that the Bible refers to both Christ and itself as "The Word of God." This is perfectly appropriate because of the strong relationship between the two.

WHAT IS THE COMPOSITION OF THE BIBLICAL BOOKS?

The Bible, as it now stands, has a unique makeup. This can be seen as follows:

Fifteen Hundred Years in the Making

From the composition of the first biblical book until the last, a period of fifteen hundred years elapsed. The Old Testament was written between 1400 and 400 B.C. The first book composed was either the Book of Genesis or the Book of Job. The books of the New Testament were written between A.D. 40 and A.D. 90.

Many Authors, Many Occupations

Over forty different human authors wrote the books of the Bible. These writers came from a variety of backgrounds and occupations. They included shepherds (Hosea and Amos) fishermen (Peter and John), a tax collector (Matthew), a prime minister (Daniel), a doctor (Luke), and a military general (Joshua).

Different Continents

The books of the Bible were composed upon three different continents, Africa, Asia, and Europe. For example, the writings of Ezekiel were composed in Babylon (Asia), Moses wrote the first five books of the Bible in the

Sinai desert (Africa), and the Apostle Paul wrote the letter to Philippi while in Rome (Europe).

Different Circumstances

There was a variety of circumstances in which the Biblical books were composed. Moses, for example, wrote while leading the children of Israel through the wilderness. Jeremiah wrote while in a dungeon in Israel. Ezekiel composed his book while a captive in Babylon. The Apostle Paul wrote several of his works while in a Roman prison. John the evangelist wrote the Book of Revelation while banished to the island of Patmos. Obviously there was not a particular place or instance in which all of the Biblical books were composed.

Though many other religions had a certain place where the "divine" word was revealed, this is not the case with the Bible. This is to point out that God could reveal Himself in many different places over an extended period of time.

Different Languages

The Bible was written in three different languages. The Old Testament was written mostly in Hebrew with some parts being composed in Aramaic; the New Testament was originally written in Greek.

Different Subjects

The Bible also covers a variety of subjects, including the existence and nature of God, the creation of the universe, the meaning of man, the purpose of existence, and the final destiny of man and the planet earth.

Hence, the Bible was written over a period of fifteen hundred years, by forty different human authors from various backgrounds who wrote in different languages, upon different continents, in different circumstances, and upon different subjects. Yet the Bible is a unity, one unfolding account from beginning to end in complete harmony and continuity. The Old Testament is incomplete without the New Testament and yet the New Testament does not make sense without the Old. Together the two testaments give a harmonious account of the dealings of God with mankind. This is one of the remarkable features of the Bible.

WHAT INFLUENCE HAS THE BIBLE HAD UPON HUMANITY?

Because the Bible claims to be God's Word written for all humanity, we ask what influence it has had since its composition. The answer is clear. Since its completion the Bible has had an influence upon our world as no other book before or since. Samuel Taylor Coleridge correctly said:

> For more than a thousand years the Bible, collectively taken, has gone hand in hand with civilization, science, law, . . . with the moral and intellectual cultivation of the species, always supporting and often leading the way.

Most Widely Read

The Bible has been read, studied, and loved more than any book in human history. Henry Van Dyke put it this way:

> Born in the East and clothed in Oriental form and imagery, the Bible walks the ways of all the world with familiar feet and enters land after land to find its own everywhere. It has learned to speak in hundreds of languages to the heart of man. Children listen to its stories with wonder and delight, and wise men ponder them as parables of life. The wicked and the proud tremble at its warnings, but to the wounded and penitent it has a mother's voice. It has woven itself into our dearest dreams; so that love, friendship, sympathy, devotion,

> memory, hope, put on beautiful garments of its treasured speech (Henry Van Dyke, *Companionable Books*, New York: Charles Scribner and Sons, n.d., p. 65).

The Bible has had this influence because it contains the testimony of Jesus Christ—which changes lives.

Most Criticized

However, the Bible has also been the most criticized book ever written. Bernard Ramm comments:

> A thousand times over, the death knell of the Bible has been sounded, the funeral procession formed, the inscription cut on the tombstone, and committal read. But somehow the corpse never stays put. No other book has been so chopped, knived, sifted, scrutinized, and vilified. What book on philosophy or religion or psychology . . . of classical or modern times has been subject to such a mass attack as the Bible? With such venom and skepticism? With such thoroughness and erudition? Upon every chapter, line, and tenet?
>
> The Bible is still loved by millions, read by millions, and studied by millions (Bernard Ramm, *Protestant Christian Evidences*, Chicago: Moody Press, 1957, p. 232,233).

We conclude that the Bible has been the most loved book in all of history as well as the most studied and criticized. It has had an influence that no other book has had upon humanity.

IN WHAT WAYS HAS THE BIBLE BEEN CRITICIZED?

The Bible has been examined by various means. The discipline of examining Scripture is known as Biblical criticism. Biblical criticism can be divided into three different categories: textual, historical, and literary.

Textual Criticism

Textual criticism has to do with establishing what each of the books of the Bible initially said. It asks, "Is the text of today the same as that which was originally written? How has the text been changed throughout history?"

Historical Criticism

The second line of criticism deals with the determination of the historical accuracy of the Bible, such as whether the Bible accurately reflects what happened in history and whether it can be trusted as a valid historical source.

Literary Criticism

The third line of criticism has to do with the authorship and sources of the Biblical book. It asks, "Was the author of the book really the person who is traditionally believed to have written it, or could someone have forged a particular book? What sources did the author use?" Literary criticism deals with these and other related questions.

Textual, historical and literary criticism are the three main ways the Bible has been criticized.

Is Biblical Criticism Valid?

Unfortunately, many who practice biblical criticism assume nothing in the Bible is true unless it is proved correct by some outside source. Scripture is assumed to be in error until some evidence can be brought up to substantiate its trustworthiness.

The opposite approach, however, should be taken. The benefit of the doubt should be given to the Bible, not to the critic, and the work should be assumed to be correct until some evidence is brought forth contradicting what has been said. This is the method used in determining the reliability of any piece of literature, whether it be ancient or modern. If any document has been transmitted in a reliable manner and demonstrates itself to be historically correct, the burden of proof is on those who question its trustworthiness.

About one hundred years ago, J. B. McClure wrote the following referring to the attacks of the famous atheist Robert Ingersoll:

> A religious faith at present so generally pervades the civilized world that it seems almost amazing that anyone should dare speak as Mr. Ingersoll does in his several lectures about the Bible. It is this singularity, no doubt, rather than intrinsic worth, which gives any significance that may attach to his words. That the Bible is in the least endangered is out of the question. It is too late now for that (J. B. McClure, *Mistakes of Ingersoll and His Answers,* Chicago: Rhodes and McClure, 1889, p. 3).

It is interesting how times have changed. McClure stated that the matter of the Bible's authority was beyond question. In the minds of the people, it has been firmly established as God's Word.

Today the opposite is the case. Most institutions of higher learning do not take the Bible seriously. Its authority on all matters of faith and practice have been severely challenged.

A Word of Warning

Sir Walter Scott wrote about those who criticize the Bible with a desire to find fault with it.

> Within that awful volume lies, the mystery
> of mysteries!
> Happiest are they of human race,
> To whom God has granted grace,
> To read to fear to hope, to pray,
> To life the latch, and force the way,
> And better had they ne'er been born,
> Who read to doubt or read to scorn.
> (*The Monastery*, ch. 12).

The criticism of the Bible is a legitimate discipline when the critic attempts to establish the text, history, and literary styles of the biblical documents. Criticism of the Bible, however, has gone far beyond that, for too many writers criticize the Bible using a different standard from the one they use with other historical documents. This is neither a scholarly or fair way of dealing with the subject.

CONCLUSION TO PART 1

As we have looked at some introductory issues concerning the Bible we can conclude the following:

1. The Bible, in both testaments, claims to be God's communication to mankind.
2. There is sufficient evidence that the Bible is exactly what it claims to be—the Word of God.
3. The Bible is necessary because human beings cannot know God from their own reasoning.
4. Scripture was written in plain language to communicate to ordinary people.
5. The Bible claims to be God's only written communication to mankind. All other revelations are false.
6. The Bible is the most influential book that has ever been written.
7. More criticism has been directed toward the Bible than any other book.
8. Because of its claims and influence, the Bible is the most important book that has ever been written.

In section 2 we will consider questions regarding the text of the Bible. Has it been transmitted accurately? Can we be assured that the Bible we read today says the same thing as it originally did? Is there any evidence that the Scripture has been changed as it has been transmitted throughout history?

PART 2

TEXTUAL CRITICISM

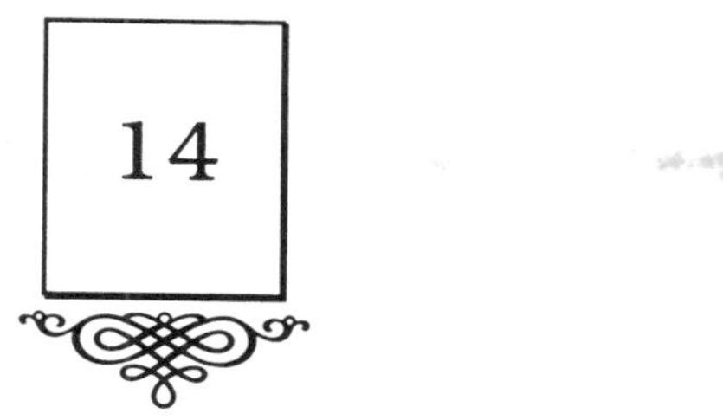

WHAT IS TEXTUAL CRITICISM?

Today, a book is printed from a manuscript that has been written by the author himself and produced under his own supervision. We can be confident that the printed form of the work accurately represents the author's original manuscript. This, however, is not the case with works written before the invention of printing. With rare exceptions the original autographs of ancient works have been lost. The texts that have survived are copies separated from the autographs by hundreds, and in some cases, thousands of years. Before we can begin to interpret these works we must first of all determine what they originally said. The science of attempting to reconstruct the text of documents is known as textual criticism.

Necessity of Textual Criticism

Textual criticism of the Bible is necessary for three reasons.

1. We do not possess any of the original writings of the Old or New Testament. We are dependent upon copies to reconstruct the text.

2. Until five hundred years ago all documents were copied by hand. The copies of the biblical manuscripts we now possess differ in some respects from each other

because of scribal mistakes that have crept into the text.

3. In the case of the New Testament there is an abundance of material to evaluate.

Before any type of biblical interpretation can begin, we must first determine what the text said. As we have mentioned, textual criticism is not limited to the Bible. The same principles of textual criticism that are applied to other works should be applied to the Bible.

The job of the textual critic is to sift through the manuscripts and carefully compare them with one another to establish the original reading of the text.

Small Percentage

It must be emphasized that in both the Old and New Testaments there are very few places where there is any question as to what the text originally said. The great majority of the Old and New Testament text reads the same in all the manuscripts. The practice of textual criticism only deals with a small percentage of the biblical text. Two of the greatest textual scholars who ever lived, Brooke Foss Westcott and Fenton John Anthony Hort, had this to say concerning the amount of variation in the New Testament manuscripts.

> If comparative trivialities, such as changes of order, the insertion or omission of an article with proper names, and the like, are set aside, the words in our opinion still subject to doubt can hardly amount to more than a thousandth part of the whole New Testament (B.F. Westcott and F.J.A. Hort, *The New Testament in Greek*, New York: MacMillan, 1957, p. 565).

We conclude that textual criticism, the establishment of the correct text, is a necessary work that needs to be performed on the Bible before interpretation can begin. The percentage of the text in which there is any question as to what it originally read is very small.

WHY DON'T WE POSSESS ANY OF THE ORIGINAL MANUSCRIPTS OF THE BOOKS OF THE BIBLE?

The original manuscripts in which the books of the Bible were written have been lost. This is true for the originals of almost all other ancient writings as well. There are several reasons why this is so.

Perishable Materials

The first reason we do not possess any of the originals of the biblical books concerns the materials upon which they were written. Surfaces such as papyri and parchment were not as durable as stone tablets. Only under the most ideal conditions can we expect this type of material to survive. Because most of the biblical text was originally written upon perishable material, we should not expect the autographs (originals) to last. J. Harold Greenlee observes,

> The autographs of the N. T. books were probably on papyrus and could hardly have survived except possibly in the dry sand of Egypt or in those conditions similar to those in the caves where the Dead Sea Scrolls have been found (J. Harold Greenlee, ibid. p. 33).

Time

The last written book of the Bible was composed some two thousand years ago. Over this long period of time manuscripts can be lost or worn out. This factor, along with the perishable surfaces of the documents, make it nearly impossible for an original text to have survived.

Texts Destroyed

Furthermore, Hebrew texts that had worn out were often destroyed when a new copy was made. The ancient scribes would meticulously copy a new manuscript from the worn out one. When the new manuscript was checked and found correct, then the old manuscript would be destroyed.

There is also the possibility that early scribes who copied New Testament manuscripts observed the Jewish practice of destroying old worn-out copies when the new ones were made. Kirsopp Lake comments:

> It is hard to resist the conclusion that the scribes usually destroyed their exemplars when they copied the Sacred Books (Kirsopp Lake, *Caesarean Text of the Gospel of Mark*. Harvard Theological Revue, Vol 21. 1928).

Object of Worship

There are some who have advocated theological reasons why the originals of the books of the Bible have not been preserved. They believe that if the originals of any books of the Bible had survived they would be made objects of worship. The faith of the believer, they contend, would be placed in the wrong object. While this is certainly possible, we cannot know whether this is true.

Due to the materials used, the long time span, the practice of destroying old copies, and possible the fact that they might become objects of worship, we do not have the original writings (autographs) of the books of the Bible. Thus the science of textual criticism is helpful and necessary in reconstructing the text from the manuscripts we do have.

UPON WHAT MATERIALS WERE THE BOOKS OF THE BIBLE ORIGINALLY WRITTEN?

One of the most ancient of all writing surfaces was stone. Job mused,

> Oh, that my words were written! Oh, that they were inscribed in a book! That they were engraved on a rock, with an iron pen and lead forever! (Job 19:23,24).

We also read of stone tablets where the commandments of God were written (Exodus 34:1).

Wooden Tablets

Some of the notes made by the prophets Habakkuk and Isaiah were perhaps upon wooden tablets:

> Then the Lord answered me and said: 'Write the vision and make it plain on tablets' (Habakkuk 2:2).

> Now go, write it before them on a tablet, and note it on a scroll, that they may be for a time to come, forever and ever (Isaiah 30:8).

Clay Tablets

Clay tablets were popular in the ancient Middle East for the straight lines of cuneiform script. However, they were not as adaptable to the Hebrew script with its curved lines. It is possible that some of the early books of the Bible, including possible sources for the Book of Genesis, were written upon clay tablets.

The above materials would only have been suitable for texts of short length. The writing of the biblical books probably employed other surfaces.

Papyrus

Papyrus is one of the most ancient writing materials known to man, used in Egypt three thousand years before Christ. This surface was made from the papyrus plant which grew in swampy areas in the delta of the Nile River. Papyrus is also referred to in the Bible:

> Can the papyrus grow up without a marsh? Can the reeds flourish without water? (Job 8:11).

Leather

Another surface used was leather. Leather scrolls had the advantage over papyrus in that they did not wear out as quickly. Of all the ancient materials used for writing, only papyrus and leather were capable of being adapted to a scroll format.

Parchment

The skins of animals were also used to receive writing in the ancient world. This is known as parchment or vellum. Parchment was the main surface used for books from the fourth century A.D. until the Middle Ages.

Paper and Printing Press

Paper began to come into use during the Middle Ages. It had been invented in the first century A.D. in China and the knowledge of its manufacture came to Europe during the eighth century.

Finally, with the invention of the printing press, the Scriptures were mass produced.

Book Forms

In the ancient world two forms of books were popular, the scroll and the codex.

The common book format of antiquity was the papyrus or leather scroll. These scrolls were made by gluing sheets of papyrus together and then winding the strips around a stick. This was a difficult form of book to work with because it required both hands: one to hold the scroll, the other hand to slowly draw out the sheets. After the scroll had been read, the reader would reroll it. Some of the scrolls were lengthy. For example, the scroll that held the sixty-six chapters of Isaiah was about twenty feet long.

The codex was made with papyrus sheets which were assembled in leaf form and written on both sides. There is good evidence that the codex was invented by Christians in the first century A.D. to arrange the different biblical books into one volume and make the passages easier to find. The parchment codex made it possible to produce many, or all, of the books of the Bible in a single volume. There are remains of papyrus codices containing Greek texts of the Old and New Testament books that have survived from the second and third centuries A.D.

HOW IS THE AGE OF A MANUSCRIPT DETERMINED?

Since there is no date printed on the outside of a written work (in ancient times), scholars use several methods to determine the age of a manuscript.

Materials

One way that the age of a manuscript can be determined is by the age of the materials upon which the document was written. The earliest writings of man were preserved in stone. As time progressed, the materials changed. Leather scrolls were used prior to the use of papyrus codices. When the ancient document is found, the materials are an important key in dating the work because of the different historical periods when these surfaces were in use.

Letter Formation

As writing progressed, the way the letters were formed changed somewhat. For example, the earliest Hebrew characters resembled pronged-shape Phoenician script. After 200 B.C. the letters were written in more square shape.

In the New Testament period, documents were first written in large letters known as uncial script. There also was no space between the words. About the tenth century, New Testament manuscripts were written in a different

Carol Moreno

WOUNDED WARRIOR PROJECT®

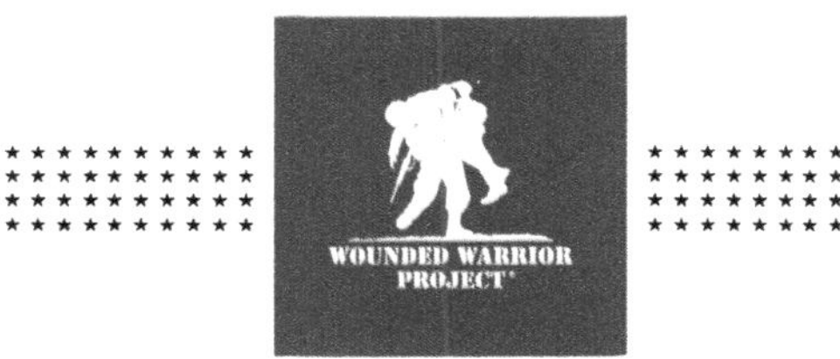

THE GREATEST CASUALTY IS BEING FORGOTTEN.®

style known as minuscule writing. This form of writing became popular and eventually all manuscripts were copied in this style.

In addition, the size and shape of letters changed as writing evolved. Certain letters were formed differently during history. Sometimes a document can be dated almost precisely, due to the way some of the letters were formed.

Punctuation

The earliest New Testament manuscripts contained no breaks between the words. About the sixth century A.D. punctuation marks began to be used. By the eighth century many different punctuation marks such as commas, colons, and periods, as well as spaces between words, were used. Since the employment was a gradual process, it helps determine the period during which a manuscript was written.

These factors, along with some others, help scholars determine the approximate time a manuscript was composed.

WHAT ABOUT SCRIBAL ERRORS IN THE MANUSCRIPTS?

Because the Old and New Testaments have been copied innumerable times in the last two thousand years, scribal errors have crept into the text.

Scribal errors arose early in the history of the New Testament text because there were few trained scribes. In addition, the majority of the people were illiterate. The scribes who did copy the text introduced changes, the majority of which were unintentional and are easily discernible as slips of the pen. These scribal errors can be broken down into two basic types: unintentional changes and intentional changes.

Unintentional Changes

Most of the changes found in the biblical manuscripts are unintentional. The following are some of the most frequent scribal errors that have crept into the text.

Errors of Sight

Sometimes a scribe misread a letter or wrongly divided a word, producing an error in the text.

Errors of Hearing

At an early date many of the Greek letters were pronounce alike. When the text was read aloud to a group of scribes who were copying the text, confusion between these letters could have occurred.

Errors of Writing

The scribe would read one thing in the text he was copying yet write another thing down in his manuscript.

Intentional Changes

There are also some intentional changes that have crept into the text. They include the following:

Grammatical Changes

In some instances the scribe changed his text because the text from which he was copying seemed grammatically incorrect. The scribe changed the word order, or the tenses of the verbs, in order to "smooth out" the text.

Elimination of Discrepancies

If the scribe through the text contained a discrepancy, then he change his manuscript to eliminate this. Ambiguous passages were sometimes clarified by "helpful" scribes. One of the most common scribal changes was to harmonize one passage with another, particularly in the Gospels.

Doctrinal Changes

Though these are rare, there are a few instances when overzealous scribes intentionally changes the text. J. Harold Greenlee writes:

> Intentional doctrinal changes which have received any appreciable [manuscript] support have almost invariably been changes in the direction of orthodoxy or stronger doctrinal emphasis. Movement toward a doctrinally weaker text is more likely an unintentional change . . . No Christian doctrine, however, hangs upon a debatable text; and the student of the N.T. must beware of wanting his text to be more doctrinally stronger than is the inspired text original (J. Harold Greenlee, *Introduction to New Testament Textual Criticism*, Grand Rapids: Eerdmans, 1964, p. 68).

Is the Text Unreliable?

Do scribal errors affect the reliability of the text? The answer is a resounding no. Only a small amount of places in the text are in dispute. New Testament scholar F.F. Bruce wrote:

> The variant readings about which any doubt remains . . . affect no material question of historic fact or of Christian faith and practice (F.F. Bruce, *The New Testament Documents: Are They Reliable?*, Grand Rapids: Eerdmans, 1954, p. 178).

Why Any Mistakes?

The question arises as to why God did not keep all the copies error-free. William Shedd wrote this concerning the mistakes found in copies.

> Why did not God inspire the copyists as well as the original authors? Why did He begin with absolute inerrancy, and end with relative inerrancy? For the same reason that, generally, He begins with the supernatural and ends with the natural. For illustration, the first founding of His Church, in both the Old and New Testament dispensation was marked by miracles; but the development of it is marked only by His operations in nature, providence and grace. the miracle was need in order to begin the kingdom of God in this sinful world, but it is not needed in order for its continuance and progress (W. T. Shedd, *Calvinism, Pure and Mixed*, New York: Charles Scribner and Sons, n.d., p. 40).

We conclude that the scribal errors that have crept into the text are minimal and do not in any way affect the message of Scripture.

WHAT DIFFERENT SOURCES ARE THERE TO THE TEXT OF THE OLD TESTAMENT?

We have already mentioned that the books of the Old Testament were composed from about 1400 to 400 B.C. and that we do not have the originals of any of the books. We are thus dependent upon copies of the originals to reconstruct the text. The major Hebrew manuscripts that textual critics use to reconstruct the original text are as follows:

The Cairo Codex of the Prophets

The Cairo Codex, also designated by the letter C for identification, contains the second division of the Hebrew Scriptures, the prophets. It was composed about A.D. 895.

The Leningrad Manuscript Heb. B 3

This manuscript, designated P for Petrograd (the former name of the Russian city of Leningrad), contains only the latter prophets. It was written in A.D. 916.

The Aleppo Manuscript

This manuscript, designated A, is from the tenth century. It contained the entire Old Testament when it was discovered, but about one fourth of the manuscript was later destroyed. There is a scribal note stating that the vowels were added by Aaron Ben Asher (died A.D. 940).

The British Museum OR 4445

This manuscript was composed about the middle of the tenth century and contains only Genesis 39:20—Deuteronomy 1:33.

The Leningrad MS. B-19 A.

Designated L, this manuscript was copied in A.D. 1008 from an earlier one prepared by Aaron Ben Moses. It contains the entire Old Testament.

These are the major surviving manuscripts of the Old Testament that scholars use to establish the correct text.

WHY DO SO FEW HEBREW MANUSCRIPTS EXIST?

There are only a few existing ancient copies of the Old Testament. The reason we do not possess many older copies of the Hebrew Scriptures is because of the reverence with which the Jews protected the purity of God's Word. The Jews considered the text so sacred that they ceremoniously disposed of worn copies. The worn copies were first stored in a special room in the synagogue, called a *Genizah*. After a number of copies accumulated, they were buried together (usually in the grave of some Jewish scholar). The Jews believed that this would protect readers from misreading God's Word because of worn spots in older manuscripts. That practice accounts for our having very few early manuscripts of the Old Testament.

Accuracy was not lost by destroying the worn copies because of the meticulous care with which the Jews copied the manuscripts. The new copy was identical to the worn-out copy in every detail.

Persecution

Manuscripts were often destroyed during medieval persecution of Jews, sometimes by their adversaries, but sometimes by the Jews themselves to prevent their Holy Scripture from falling into the hand of infidels. This also contributed to the lack of manuscripts.

Meticulous Copying Procedures

Because of their reverence for the Word of God, the Jews were not allowed to produce mass copies of Scripture. The copying processes were meticulous, and thus there were fewer copies made. Samuel Davidson lists the minute regulations that the Jewish scribes employed:

1. A synagogue roll must be written on the skins of clean animals,
2. prepared for the particular use of the synagogue by a Jew.
3. These must be fastened together with strings taken from certain clean animals.
4. Each skin must contain a certain number of columns, equal throughout the entire codex.
5. The length of each column must not extend over less than forty-eight or more than sixty lines; and the breadth must consist of thirty letters.
6. The whole copy must be first-lined; and if three words be written without a line, it is worthless.
7. The ink should be black, neither red, green, nor any other color, and be prepared according to a definite recipe.
8. An authentic copy must be from an exemplar, from which the transcriber ought not in the least deviate.
9. No word or letter, not even a yod, must be written from memory, the scribe not having looked at the codex before him
10. Between every consonant the space of a hair or thread must intervene;
11. Between every new . . . section, the breadth of nine consonants;
12. Between every book, three lines.
13. The fifth book of Moses must terminate exactly with a line; but the rest need not do so.
14. Besides this, the copyist must sit in full Jewish dress,
15. Wash his whole body,
16. Not begin to write the name of God with a pen newly dipped in ink,
17. And should a king address him while writing that name he must take no notice of him (Samuel Davidson, *The Hebrew Text of the Old Testament*, 2nd ed., London: Samuel Bagster and Sons, 1859, p. 89).

Therefore, the lack of numerous Hebrew manuscripts of the Old Testament does not take away from the reliability of the text.

WHAT ARE THE DEAD SEA SCROLLS?

Until recently, the only complete manuscripts we possessed to reconstruct the text of the Old Testament came from A.D. 900, some fourteen hundred years after the Old Testament was completed. But the situation changed with the discovery of the Dead Sea Scrolls.

What Are They?

The "Dead Sea Scrolls" is the popular term for the manuscripts discovered in 1947 in caves about five hundred yards from the Dead Sea. The scrolls are the writings of a community that lived alongside the Dead Sea from approximately 150 B.C. to A.D. 70. Some manuscripts date back to 100 B.C. Among the manuscripts discovered were portions of every Old Testament book except Esther.

Value

The value of the Dead Sea Scrolls is that we can see how the Hebrew text read one hundred years before the time of Christ. Until the time of their discovery, the earliest complete manuscript of the Old Testament came from about A.D. 1000. Scholars finally could check the faithfulness in which the text had been copied between the time of 100 B.C. and A.D. 1000.

The Dead Sea Scrolls confirm that the scribes copying the Old Testament text were faithful to the task. The copies of the Old Testament books found among the Dead Sea Scrolls read substantially the same as those written in A.D. 1000. This caused the Old Testament authority Millar Burrows to write,

> It is a matter for wonder that through something like a thousand years that the text went through so little alteration (Millar Burrows, *Burrows on the Dead Sea Scrolls*, Grand Rapids: Baker Book House, 1981, p. 304).

We conclude that the discovery of the Dead Sea Scrolls demonstrated the faithfulness of the Hebrew scribes in their copying of the text.

WHAT IS THE SEPTUAGINT?

One of the most important translations with regard to the Bible is known as the Septuagint.

History

Septuagint is the Greek word for seventy, and thus it is often abbreviated by the Roman numeral LXX. The history behind the Septuagint is uncertain. About one hundred years before Christ, a letter surfaced claiming to have been written some 150 years earlier (ca. 250 B.C.). The author was Arestias, an underling to Ptolemy Philadelphus (285-245 B.C.) of Egypt. From the letter of Arestias we find a fanciful account of the translation of the Hebrew Old Testament into Greek. Supposedly seventy-two scholars, six from each Jewish tribe, translated the first five books of the Bible from Hebrew into Greek in seventy-two days. According to Arestias, though they were in the separate rooms, all seventy-two translations were in exact agreement!

More likely, the translation began about 250 B.C. with the translation of the Torah, the first five Old Testament books, from Hebrew to Greek.

Importance

The Septuagint is important for several reasons. It was the earliest attempt to translate a large work from one language to another. Because it was translated some two centuries before Christ, it testifies to the way the text of the Old Testament read at the time. Scholars use the Septuagint to learn about the Hebrew text that the work was translated from.

Testimony to Masoretic Text

The verdict from the examination of the Septuagint is a confirmation of the traditional Masoretic text of the Old Testament. The conclusion from the study of the Septuagint is that the traditionally accepted Hebrew text was one in use at the time of this translation.

HAS THE TEXT OF THE OLD TESTAMENT BEEN TRANSMITTED IN A RELIABLE MANNER?

The Hebrew text used for translation into other languages is called "Masoretic" because its present form is based upon the Masora, the textual traditions of Jewish scholars known as the Masoretes. The first complete Hebrew manuscript that contains the entire Old Testament dates from the tenth century A.D. We know we can trust the accuracy of the traditional Masoretic text for the following reasons.

Fewer Manuscripts

Few Old Testament manuscripts have survived. Yet even with fewer manuscripts, we can still be confident that the Old Testament text has been accurately transmitted. With regard to the Old Testament manuscripts, age is not the sole or primary criterion because of the meticulous regulations laid down to copyists.

There are also few variations in the masoretic text. The reason the variations are few is because of the reverence the people had for the text. Consequently, official scribes were used to copy the text, abiding by strict rules.

Old Testament scholar Bruce Waltke comments on the psychology of scribes in the ancient world:

> Both the Bible itself (cf. Deuteronomy 31: 9ff; Joshua 24: 25-26; 1 Samuel 10:25) and the literature of the ancient near East show that at the time of its earliest composition a psychology of canonicity existed. This psychology must have fostered a concern for the care and accuracy in transmission of the sacred writings. For example, a treaty of the Hittite international suzerainty treaties parallel to Yahweh's covenant with Israel at Sinai contains this explicit threat: 'Whoever changes but one word of this tablet, may the weather god . . . and the thousand gods of this tablet root the man's descendants out of the land of Hatti:' Likewise one of the Sefire Steles (c. 750 B.C.) reads, 'Whoever . . . says, I will efface some of its words, . . . may the gods throw over that man and his house and all in it.' Again, in the conclusion of the famous code of Hammurabi, imprecations are hurled against those who would try to alter the law. And Moses insisted that Israel 'observe all these laws with care' (Deuteronomy 31:12). Undoubtedly this psychology, coupled with a fear for God in the heart of the scribes, who did their work in connection with ark, inhibited them from multiplying variants of the text (Bruce Waltke in Biblical *Criticism*, R.K. Harrison, ed. Grand Rapids: Zondervan, 1978, pp. 49,50).

Dead Sea Scrolls

The Dead Sea Scrolls, which contain Hebrew manuscripts dating from 100 B.C., confirm the reliability of the traditional Masoretic text. When the texts are compared, the variation between the two is slight.

We must emphasize that the Hebrews, in particular, had a reverence for their text. Flavius Josephus, a Jewish writer living in the first century A.D. testified to the care the Hebrews took in copying their sacred text.

> We have been given practical proof of our reverence for our own Scriptures. For, although such long ages have now passed, no one has ventured either to add, or to remove, or to alter a syllable; and it is instinct with every Jew, from the day of his birth, to regard them as the decrees of God, to abide by them, an if need be, cheerfully die for them. Time and time again ere now the sight has been witnessed of prisoners enduring tortures and death in every form in the theatres, rather than utter a single word against the laws and the allied documents (Flavius Josephus, "Against Apion," in *Josephus' Complete Works*, William Whiston, trans., Grand Rapids, Kregel Publications, 1960, pp. 179,180).

One of the great Old Testament scholars of our century, Robert Dick Wilson, affirmed that the evidence is in favor of the accuracy of the Old Testament text. He declared:

> In 144 cases of transliteration from Egyptian, Assyrian, Babylonian and Moabite into Hebrew and in 40 cases of the opposite, or 184 in all, the evidence shows that for 2300 to 3900 years the text of the proper names in the Hebrew Bible has been transmitted with the most minute accuracy. That the original scribes should have written them with such close conformity to correct philological principles is a wonderful proof of their thorough care and scholarship; further, that the Hebrew text should have been transmitted by copyists through so many centuries is a phenomenon unequaled in the history of literature . . . There are about forty of these [Old Testament] kings living from 2000 B.C. to 400 B.C. Each appears in chronological order . . . with reference to the kings of the same country with respect to kings of other countries . . . no stronger evidence for the substantial accuracy of the Old Testament records could possibly be imagined, than this collection of kings. Mathematically, it is one chance in 750,000,000,000,000,000,000,000 that this accuracy is mere circumstance . . . The proof that the copies of the original documents have been handed down with substantial correctness for more than 2000 years cannot be denied (Robert Dick Wilson, *A Scientific Investigation of the Old Testament,* Chicago, Moody Press, 1959, pp. 70, 71, 85).

The evidence is clear that the Old Testament has been transmitted to us in an accurate manner.

WHAT ARE THE DIFFERENT SOURCES TO THE TEXT OF THE NEW TESTAMENT?

As we have already noted, the autographs (originals) of the New Testament have long since perished. Even if by some miraculous discovery an original were found, its genuineness would still need to be determined. Thus, we are left with manuscript copies, and copies of copies, to establish what the New Testament originally said. The evidence for the New Testament text can be divided into three different groups: the Greek manuscripts, the translations or versions, and the writings of the church fathers.

Greek Manuscripts

Greek was the language in which all the books of the New Testament were originally written. The Greek manuscripts are the first source that the textual critic examines in order to reconstruct what the text originally said because (1) it is the original language of the New Testament authors, and (2) the oldest Greek manuscripts were generally written earlier than the versions and the writings of the church fathers.

Versions

The versions are translations from one language to another. Christianity, from its inception, was a missionary religion, and at an early date the New Testament Scriptures were translated into other languages. These versions are a secondary source because they are translations at least once removed from the original Greek text. Furthermore, the versions must also undergo textual criticism.

Church Fathers

The writings of the early Christians known as church fathers, constitute another source of testimony to the New Testament documents. They wrote commentaries, defenses of Christianity, personal letters, and other materials that contained references to the New Testament. As is true with the versions, the writings of the church fathers must also undergo textual criticism.

These three sources, Greek manuscripts, translations into other languages (versions) and the writing of the church fathers are the tools the textual critic uses to reconstruct the text of the New Testament.

HOW MANY ANCIENT MANUSCRIPTS OF THE NEW TESTAMENT STILL EXIST?

We have seen that there are basically three different sources from which the New Testament can be reconstructed. Each of these sources has many manuscripts that need to be evaluated. The numbering of the manuscripts is as follows:

Greek Manuscripts

The Greek manuscripts can be divided into four different categories: papyri, uncial, minuscule and lectionaries.

Papyri

The oldest manuscripts in which the New Testament was written are found on papyri. These manuscripts were written in uncial script using large, upper-case letters with no separation between words. Papyrus is perishable material, so there have been relatively few papyrus manuscripts (92) catalogued.

Uncial

At the beginning of the fourth century, parchment began to replace papyrus as the most often used writing material. The scribes continued to write in the uncial script but were now writing on more durable, longer-lasting material. Uncial manuscripts were popular until the ninth century. There are 268 uncial manuscripts catalogued.

Minuscule

Minuscule, or cursive, manuscripts, were popular from the ninth to the sixteenth century. Because this style of writing could produce manuscripts faster, it soon replaced the more deliberate uncial script. There have been 2,792 minuscule manuscripts catalogued.

Lectionaries

Lectionary manuscripts are Scripture portions that were used for daily or weekly lessons in the church. There are 2,193 lectionary manuscripts catalogued, containing both uncial and minuscule styles of writing.

When we total up the various Greek manuscripts, it comes to over 5,500.

Versions

As Christianity spread, the New Testament was translated into many other languages. The manuscript evidence from different versions is enormous. At least 10,000 manuscripts containing some part of the New Testament text still exist in Latin. The total number of manuscripts may be as high as 25,000. Manuscripts from other versions such as Syriac and Armenian total several more thousand.

Church Fathers

The citations from the fathers are likewise numerous. The quotations of the church fathers are so numerous that the entire text of the New Testament could be reconstructed from the writings of the church fathers who lived before A.D. 325. At the end of the last century, textual scholar John Burgon catalogued over 86,000 separate references to the New Testament in the writings of people before the fourth century.

Not Necessarily Complete

When we speak of manuscripts, we are not necessarily speaking of complete manuscripts. For example, of 5,500 Greek manuscripts, about 200 are complete, another 50 contain the entire New Testament except the Gospels, and about 1,500 contain all or part of the Gospels alone.

When the evidence from the witnesses to the New Testament text is considered, we discover that the New Testament text can be established with confidence. Even the least attested New Testament book, Revelation, has over 300 Greek manuscripts containing its text. No other ancient book has anywhere near the amount of manuscript testimony as the New Testament.

HAS THE NEW TESTAMENT BEEN TRANSMITTED IN A RELIABLE MANNER?

We know that the New Testament has come down to us in a reliable manner for the following reasons:

Short Time Span

There was a short time span between when the New Testament was originally written and the earliest copies. The books of the New Testament were composed between A.D. 50 and A.D. 90. The earliest complete manuscript that has survived from A.D. 325. In addition, there are over fifty other manuscripts written before that time that still exist. All things being equal, the shorter the time, the better the chance of reproducing the original without errors creeping into the text.

Abundance of Manuscripts

The number of manuscripts available to reconstruct the text of the New Testament is greater than all other writings of the ancient world. We have seen that between the Greek manuscripts and various versions, there are over 24,000 manuscripts of the New Testament. The more manuscripts the textual critic has to work with, the surer he becomes of reconstructing the original text.

When the manuscripts are compared with one another, there is no substantial variation. They all give the same basic account. From the earliest manuscripts until the present, there has not been any substantial change in the text.

These three facts: (1) the short time span between the original and the manuscript copies (2) the great number of manuscripts, and (3) the lack of any substantial variation between the manuscripts, demonstrate that the New Testament can be trusted. Sir Frederic Kenyon, the former principal librarian and director of the British Museum, was an authority second to none on New Testament textual criticism. He had this to say concerning the reliability of the New Testament text:

> The interval between the dates of original composition (of the New Testament) and the earliest extant evidence becomes so small as to be in fact negligible, and the last foundation for any doubt that the Scriptures have come down to us substantially as they were written has now been removed. Both the authenticity and general integrity of the books of the New Testament may be regarded as finally established (Sir Frederic Kenyon, *The Bible and Archaeology*, New York, Harper and Row, 1940, pp. 288,289).

HOW DOES THE NEW TESTAMENT COMPARE TO OTHER ANCIENT WORKS?

When the New Testament text is compared with that of other ancient works it far exceeds them in reliability.

Shorter Time Span

The time span between the original composition of the New Testament and the earliest existing manuscripts is much smaller than other ancient works. For example, there is a period of 1,100 years between the time Caesar wrote *The Gallic Wars* and the earliest surviving manuscript used to reconstruct the text. Other ancient writers also have long periods of time between the original composition of the document and the first surviving copy. For example, in the case of Homer's *Iliad* there is a 500-year time span. With the Latin poet Catullus, there is a 1,500 year time span. As we have seen with the New Testament, there is a period of less than 250 years between the time it was originally written and the earliest existing complete copy. Over fifty manuscript fragments can be found between the time of the New Testament's composition and A.D. 325.

More Manuscripts

The 24,000-plus manuscripts of the New Testament greatly surpass the amount of manuscript evidence for other ancient works. Textual scholar J. Harold Greenlee writes:

> The plays of Aeschylus are known in some fifty mss., the works of Sophocles in one hundred, the Greek Anthology of the Annals of Tacitus in one ms. each, the poems of Catullus in three mss. . . . Since scholars accept as generally trustworthy the writings of the ancient classics, even though the earliest mss. were written so long after the original writings, and the number of extant mss. is in many instances so small, it is clear that the reliability of the text of the N.T. is likewise assured (J. Harold Greenlee, *Introduction to New Testament Criticism*, Grand Rapids: Eerdmans, 1964, p. 16).

Comparison to Shakespeare

William Shakespeare wrote thirty-seven plays in the seventeenth century, all after the invention of printing. The originals have not survived. In every one of his plays there are gaps in the printed text where we do not know what was originally written. Textual scholars attempt to fill in the gaps in the printed copies by making an educated guess as to what the text said. The New Testament, written some sixteen centuries earlier, is in much better textual shape. Because of the abundance of manuscript evidence, there is not one portion of the text of the New Testament wherein we must guess what was originally written.

We conclude that the New Testament's text is in better shape than classical works because:

1. The time interval between the original composition and the earliest copied manuscripts is much shorter than with other ancient works.

2. The number of manuscripts for the New Testament far outnumber the manuscripts existing from any other ancient author.

WHAT ABOUT ALL THE VARIANT READINGS IN THE MANUSCRIPTS?

Some have objected to the New Testament as being a reliable document due to all the variants in the manuscripts.

What Are Variants?

A variant reading can be defined as any place in the text where two given manuscripts disagree with each other. For example, in John 1:18 there is a variant with regard to a description of Christ. Some manuscripts read the "only begotten Son" while other manuscripts read the "only begotten God." Therefore, we have a variant in the manuscripts. Whenever two manuscripts disagree with regard to word order, spelling, grammar, etc. it constitutes a variant.

Few variations in the text actually exist. There is complete agreement among the manuscripts in about 95 percent of the text. The 5 percent where there is any question consists mostly of trivialities such as word order and spelling.

Doesn't Affect Christian Doctrine

As we have seen, the variants do not materially affect the meaning of the text, and so Christian doctrine is not affected by text variations. The introduction to the Revised Standard Version of the Bible says,

> It will be obvious to the careful reader that still in 1946 as in 1881 and 1901, no doctrine of the Christian faith has been affected by the revision, for the simple reason that, out of the thousands of variant readings in the manuscripts, none has turned up thus far that requires a revision of Christian doctrine (F.C. Grant, "An Introduction to the Revised Standard Version of the New Testament," *The New Testament, Revised Standard Version*, Nashville: Thomas Nelson, 1946, p. 42).

The great textual scholar, Sir Frederic Kenyon, wrote,

> The number of manuscripts of the New Testament, of early translations from it, and of quotations from it in the oldest writers of the Church, is so large that it is practically certain that the true reading of every doubtful passage is preserved in some one or other of these ancient authorities. This can be said of no other book in the world (Sir Frederic Kenyon, *Our Bible and Ancient Manuscripts*, New York: Harper and Brothers, 1941, p. 55).

We can rightly conclude that the variations in the different manuscripts have no affect whatsoever on the reliability of the text or upon Christian theology.

WHAT ARE THE OLDEST EXISTING NEW TESTAMENT MANUSCRIPTS?

Since we do not have in our possession the originals (autographs) of any of the books of the New Testament, we may ask about the manuscripts that do exist. Where can the oldest ones be found?

John Rylands Manuscript

The oldest manuscript that contains any part of the New Testament is a small fragment known as p^{52} or the John Rylands manuscript. The *p* stands for papyrus and the number "52" means it is the fifty-second papyrus manuscript of the New Testament that has been catalogued. The fragment contains John 18:31-33 on the front and John 18:37-38 on the back. This small scrap has been dated from A.D. 100-140 and is housed in the John Rylands Library in Manchester, England.

Bodmer Papyrus

The Bodmer papyrus is a collection of manuscripts housed in the Bodmer Library in Geneva, Switzerland. They include:

p^{66}, which dates from A.D. 150 and contains a large portion of the Gospel of John.

p72, which dates from the third century and contains, among other things, 1 and 2 Peter and Jude.

p75, which dates toward the end of the second century and contains a lengthy part of the Gospels of Luke and John.

Chester Beatty Papyri

The Chester Beatty papyri comes from the Chester Beatty collection and can be found variously in Dublin, Ireland and at the University of Michigan.

p45, This manuscript dates from the early third century and contains one-seventh of the text of the Gospels and Acts.

Codex Sinaiticus

Codex Sinaiticus, also known by the Hebrew letter א *aleph*, is a fourth century manuscript housed in the British Museum. This manuscript was discovered a century ago by Constantine Tischendorf on Mt. Sinai (hence Sinaiticus). It contains the complete Old and New Testaments.

A (02) Codex Alexandrinus

Alexandrinus is a fifth-century manuscript also kept in the British Museum. It contains most of both Testaments. The New Testament is complete except for most of Matthew, 2 Corinthians, and part of the Gospel of John.

B (03) Codex Vaticanus

Vaticanus dates from about A.D. 325. It contains most of both Testaments, lacking only parts of Hebrews and all of Titus, Philemon, and Revelation. It has resided for the last 500 years in the Vatican library.

C (04) Codex Ephraemi Rescriptus

This fifth-century manuscript contains almost the entire New Testament. It is a palimpsest. This means the original text was scraped off and something else was written over it. Through the use of chemical agents the erased portion of the text can be restored. Today it resides at the *Bibliotheque Nationale* in Paris.

D (05) Codex Bezae

A sixth-century manuscript of the Gospels and Acts, is located in the Cambridge library in England.

D *Paul* (06) Codex Claramontanus

This sixth-century manuscript, containing the letters of Paul, and the Book of Hebrews, resides in the *Bibliotheque Nationale* in Paris. Like Codex Bezae, it is a bilingual manuscript, having Greek and Latin on facing pages.

W (032) Codex Freericanus or Washingtonensis

This fourth-century manuscript is located at the Freer Art Gallery of the Smithsonian Institute in Washington, D. C.

These are the major surviving manuscripts of the New Testament which the textual critic uses to establish the correct text.

WHAT IS THE TEXTUS RECEPTUS?

When people speak of the manuscripts that lie behind the text of the New Testament, the term *Textus Receptus* or "received text" often comes up. The *Textus Receptus* is basically the same Greek text as the one used in translating the King James Version of the Bible, differing in only 287 places. It received its name from a publisher's blurb in the second edition of the Greek New Testament published by the Elzevir brothers in Holland in 1633. The publishers proclaimed it as "the text which is now received by all, in which we give nothing changed or corrupted." It was the text "received by all" because it was the only text available to all! The text was based on less than ten Greek manuscripts dated before the ninth century A.D.

Other Discoveries

Since the time of the Textus Receptus, other more ancient manuscripts have been found. Some fifteen years after the King James Version was first translated in 1611, a fifth-century manuscript, Codex Alexandrinus, was brought to England. Today over 5,500 Greek manuscripts have been catalogued, with some dating as early as the second century. These ancient manuscripts are extremely valuable in New Testament textual criticism and help the textual critic establish the original text of the New Testament.

CONCLUSION TO PART 2

After examining the subject of the textual criticism of the Bible we can make several conclusions.

1. Textual Criticism is a science attempting to establish the correct text of a document. It is applied to secular as well as sacred works.

2. The Old Testament, though having few surviving manuscripts, has been transmitted accurately. This is due to the reverence the Jews had toward the text they were copying.

3. The New Testament, with its abundance of existing manuscripts, overwhelms all other ancient works in the number of manuscripts available to reconstruct the text.

4. There is a relatively short time span between the original composition of the New Testament and the earliest available manuscripts to reconstruct the text.

5. We can, therefore, rest assured that the text we read today accurately represents what was originally written in both the Old and New Testaments.

Our next section deals with the historical accuracy of the Bible. Do the events of history match those recorded in Scripture? Is it important that the Bible is historically accurate? Was the New Testament written soon after the events it records? We will consider these and other important issues as we examine the historical accuracy of Scripture.

PART 3

HISTORICAL ACCURACY

IS IT IMPORTANT THAT THE BIBLE IS HISTORICALLY ACCURATE?

It is of utmost importance that the revelation of God to man was accomplished through His mighty words and deeds in history.

The Bible is a testimony of the mighty works of God. The Lord reminded His people of this.

> I am the Lord your God, who brought you out of the land of Egypt, out of the house of bondage (Exodus 20:2).

Urged to Remember

The nation was continually urged to remember these deeds of God:

> But the Lord, who brought you up from the land of Egypt with great power and an outstretched arm . . . Him you shall worship (2 Kings 17:36).

> O My people, remember now . . . that you may know the righteousness of the Lord (Micah 6:5).

God Came to Our World

Jesus Christ, God the Son, came into our world.

> And the Word became flesh and dwelt among us, and we beheld His glory, the glory as of the only begotten of the Father, full of grace and truth (John 1:14).

We see the writers of Scripture appealing time and time again to actual historical events to testify to the power and existence of God. The entire biblical revelation centers on what God did in history.

Important Issue

Some people say that the message of Scripture is what is important, not whether the Bible is historically accurate. Such is not the case, however, as attorney/theologian John Warwick Montgomery writes:

> Christianity's truth claim to truth consists merely of a finger pointing back through time to an historical figure who divided world history into two parts—to Jesus of Nazareth—to His statements concerning Himself and true religion, and to the life He led attesting to the statements He made. An honest, historically accurate, scientific investigation of these data (involving chiefly a study of the documents collected in the New Testament) will show that Jesus claimed to be God Incarnate, that He described the only true (but not the only possible) religion consisting of fellowship with Himself, and that He attested His claims by a sinless life which profoundly affected everyone who crossed His path, and by a resurrection which left no doubt in the minds of eyewitnesses that He was in fact the true God (John Warwick Montgomery, *The Shape of The Past: An Introduction to Philosophical Historiography*, vol. 1, Ann Arbor, Mich., 1962, p. 328).

Must Demonstrate to be Factual

The Bible must be able to withstand the most thorough historical investigation. Millar Burrows, who was America's foremost expert on the Dead Sea Scrolls wrote,

> There is a type of Christian faith, . . . rather strongly represented today, [that] regards the affirmation of Christian faith as confessional statements which the individual accepts as a member of the believing community, and which are not dependent on reason or evidence. Those who hold this position will not admit that historical investigation can have anything to say about the uniqueness of Christ. they are often skeptical as to

> the possibility of knowing anything about the historical Jesus . . . I cannot share this point of view. I am profoundly convinced that the historic revelation of God in Jesus of Nazareth must be the cornerstone of any faith that is really Christian. Any historical question about the real Jesus who lived in Palestine nineteen centuries ago is therefore fundamentally important (Millar Burrows, *More Light on the Dead Sea Scrolls*, New York: Viking Press, 1958, p. 55).

The historical accuracy of Scripture is of vital importance, for it is the appeal made by the Bible itself to argue for its truthfulness. The evidence, as we will see, demonstrates that the Bible is accurate when speaking about matters of history.

WHEN WERE THE FOUR GOSPELS WRITTEN?

The Bible contains four different books, Matthew, Mark, Luke, and John, that give a first-hand account of the life and ministry of Jesus Christ.

These works are known as the gospels. When were they written? Can we trust their portrait of Jesus?

Early Date

The evidence shows that the four Gospels were written in a relatively short time after the death and resurrection of Jesus Christ. The first three Gospels, and possibly also the fourth were apparently written while the city of Jerusalem was still standing. Each of the first three Gospels contain predictions by Jesus concerning the destruction of Jerusalem, but none records the fulfillment. We know that the city of Jerusalem was destroyed by Titus the Roman in A.D. 70. Hence, the composition of the first three Gospels must have occurred sometime before this event.

Acts

The Book of Acts also provides us with a clue as to when the Gospels were written. Acts records the highlights in the life and ministry of the Apostle Paul. The book concludes with Paul at Rome awaiting trial before Caesar. The inference is that Acts was written while Paul was still alive, since his death is not recorded. There is good evidence that Paul died in the Neronian persecution about A.D. 67. If Acts were written before that date, then this also helps us date the Gospels, since the Book of Acts is the second half of a treatise written by Luke to Theophilus. Since we know that the gospel of Luke was written before the Book of Acts, we can then date the Gospel of Luke sometime around A.D. 60, based on the assumption that Paul was still alive when it was composed.

Mark First

Furthermore, modern scholarship has generally assumed that the Gospel of Mark was written before Luke. If this is the case, then we are somewhere in the fifties of the first century when this book was composed. Since Jesus' death and resurrection occurred about A.D. 30, the Gospels were written during the time when eyewitnesses both friendly and unfriendly, were still alive could verify or falsify the Gospel record of Jesus.

Therefore, the evidence leads us to conclude that the Gospels were written at an early date, soon after the life of Christ.

WHEN WERE THE LETTERS OF PAUL COMPOSED?

We have seen that the Gospels were written a relatively short time after the death and resurrection of Christ. What about the letters of the Apostle Paul? When were they composed?

Some of the letters of the Apostle Paul were composed earlier than the Gospels. For example, 1 Thessalonians was written approximately A.D. 51, while the first letter to the Corinthians was penned about A.D. 56. Obviously, all thirteen of his letters were written before A.D. 67, when he died.

Confirmed Gospel Accounts

The testimony of the Apostle Paul confirms the evidence presented by the Gospel accounts concerning Jesus Christ. Paul taught the following concerning Jesus.

Creator of the Universe

Paul testified that Jesus was the Creator of the universe:

> For by Him all things were created that are in heaven and that are on the earth, visible and invisible, whether thrones or dominions or principalities or powers. All things were created through Him and for Him (Colossians 1:16).

Obeyed the Jewish Law

Paul emphasized that Jesus was obedient to the Old Testament law,

> But when the fullness of the time had come, God sent forth His Son, born of a woman, born under the law (Galatians 4:4).

Betrayed

Paul spoke of Jesus' betrayal by Judas:

> For I received from the Lord that which I also delivered to you; that the Lord Jesus on the same night in which He was betrayed took bread (1 Corinthians 11:23).

Crucified

Paul mentions Jesus' death by crucifixion as the cornerstone of his message: "But we preach Christ crucified" (1 Corinthians 1:23).

Rose from the Dead

Paul also confirmed that Christ rose from the dead:

> For I delivered to you first of all that which I also received: that Christ died for ours sins, according to the Scriptures, and that He was buried, and that He rose again the third day, according to the Scriptures (1 Corinthians 15:3,4).

Three points must be emphasized concerning the testimony of Paul.

Contemporary of the Disciples

The Apostle Paul, though not an eyewitness to the events of the life of Christ, was living at the same time as the disciples who were eyewitnesses.

Wrote Within Thirty years of the Events

Paul's letters were composed within thirty years of the events of the life and ministry of Jesus. This is far too short a time for him to have radically changed the message of Jesus without receiving criticism from believing and non-believing eyewitnesses of the events.

Challenged his Readers to Investigate the Evidence

Paul challenged his readers to investigate for themselves the evidence concerning the resurrection of Jesus Christ. He wrote to the church in Corinth about the resurrected Christ.

> He was seen by over five hundred brethren at once, of whom the greater part remain to the present (1 Corinthians 15:6).

Many eyewitnesses to Jesus' resurrection were still alive when Paul wrote to the church at Corinth. Anyone doubting the fact of the resurrection could check out their testimony.

We conclude that the testimony of the Apostle Paul adds further evidence to the trustworthiness of the Gospel's picture of Jesus.

HOW SOON AFTER THE LIFE OF JESUS WAS THE NEW TESTAMENT COMPOSED?

Were the writers of the New Testament familiar with the events they recorded or were they merely citing the testimony of others?

The following quotation is typical of many people who are unaware of the facts:

> We can show that the oldest New Testament texts come from at least two centuries after the events they relate. Using the New Testament to substantiate events of the first century C.E. [Christian Era] then, is analogous to reconstructing the life of George Washington based on books not in print before 1957. And which exist only in translation. Scholars largely agree that Jesus did not speak in the Greek of the New Testament, and while stories may 'lose' in translation, they can also 'gain.' Moreover the New Testament was not canonized until 367 C.E., plenty of time for editors to make whatever changes their piety declared (Stanley N. Rosenbaum, "Jews for Jesus: Causes and Treatment," *Midstream*, December 1985, p. 12).

This statement is totally in error, showing complete ignorance of the facts.

First-Century Authorship

William F. Albright, one of the greatest archaeologists who ever lived, stated,

> We can already say emphatically that there is no longer any solid basis for dating any book of the New Testament after A.D. 80, two full generations before the date between 130 and 150 given by the radical critics of today (W.F. Albright, *Recent Discoveries in Bible Lands*, New York: Funk and Wagnalls, 1955, p. 136).

Why is this important? The matter of the composition of the text is extremely important, because if the documents were written and circulated at an early date they eyewitnesses would still be living who could verify or deny the events recorded.

Testimony of Unbelievers

It is interesting to note that even unbelievers have unwittingly testified to Scripture's authenticity. Speaking of Celsus, a man living in the second century who hated Christianity, Bishop Fallows writes,

> This unbeliever, although he caused great annoyance to the believers in Christ living in his day, and seemed to be disturbing the foundations of the Christian faith, rendered more real service to Christianity than any father of undisputed orthodoxy in the Church. He admits all the grand facts and doctrines of the gospel, as they were preached by the Apostles, and contained in the acknowledged writings, for the sake of opposing. He makes in his attacks eighty quotations from the New Testament, and appeals to it as containing the sacred writings of Christians, universally received by them as credible and Divine.
>
> He is, therefore, the very best witness we can summon to prove that the New Testament was not written hundreds of years after the Apostles were dust; but in less than a century and a half had been received by the Christian Church all over the world. He expressly quotes both the synoptic Gospels, as they were termed (the first three Gospels), and the Gospel of St. John. (Bishop Fallows, *Mistakes of Ingersoll and His Answers*, pp. 91,92).

Consequently, the evidence is that the New Testament documents were written soon after the events they record.

COULD THE NEW TESTAMENT WRITERS HAVE HAD FAULTY MEMORIES?

If we grant that the New Testament was composed at an early date what about the possibility that the writers had a faulty memory of what occurred?

Memory Culture

The people in the first century were not as literate as modern man. Consequently, they relied more upon memory than we do today. John Warwick Montgomery makes an appropriate comment:

> We know from the Mishna that it was Jewish custom to memorize a Rabbi's teaching, for a good pupil was like 'a plastered cistern that loses not a drop' [Mishna Aboth II.8]. And we can be sure that the early Church, impressed as it was with Jesus governed itself by this ideal (John Warwick Montgomery, *History and Christianity*, Downers Grove, Ill.: Intervarsity Press, 1964, pp. 37,38).

Written Soon After the Events

We are not dealing with generations but rather a short period of time between the happening of the events and their recording. The late John A.T. Robinson, a liberal scholar, in his book redating the New Testament, concluded there is sufficient evidence for believing that every New Testament book was composed before the fall of Jerusalem in A.D. 70.

Made a Vivid Impression

The events of the life of Christ would have made a vivid impression on all of the people who witnessed them. Miracles were not the norm and any extraordinary event would not be soon forgotten. After Jesus head a paralyzed man the Bible records the reaction of the people:

> Immediately he arose, took up the bed, and went out in the presence of them all, so that all were amazed and glorified God, saying, 'We never saw anything like this!' (Mark 2:12).

Number of Eyewitnesses

The number of eyewitnesses to the miracles of Christ were sufficient. The Apostle Paul said that the resurrection of Christ was witnessed by over five hundred people at one time:

> After that He was seen by over five hundred brethren at once, of whom the greater part remain to the present, but some have fallen asleep (1 Corinthians 15:6).

Not All Were Believers

It must be remembered that not all of the eyewitnesses to the Biblical miracles were believers. If the disciples tended to distort the facts; the unbelieving eyewitnesses would have immediately objected.

Hypothesis Fails

These reasons demonstrate that the faulty memory hypothesis does not fit the facts. The New Testament was composed in such a short time after the events occurred that it would be folly to assume that the writers' memories were so faulty that neither they nor the unbelievers could remember the actual events of the life of Christ.

WHY SHOULD WE RELY UPON THE NEW TESTAMENT ACCOUNT OF THE LIFE OF JESUS?

The first reason we should believe them is that the New Testament writers were eyewitnesses.

> That which was from the beginning, which we have heard, which we have seen with our eyes, which we have looked upon, and our hands have handled, concerning the Word of Life . . . that which we have seen and heard we declare to you (1 John 1:1,3).

They were there!

Knew the Difference

The New Testament writers also knew the difference between myth and reality:

> For we did not follow cunningly devised fables when we made known to you the power and coming of our Lord Jesus Christ, but we were eyewitnesses of His majesty (2 Peter 1:16).

Because they were eyewitnesses, they were in a better position to recount the life and teachings of Jesus than anyone else.

Consistent

The testimony of the various Gospel writers is consistent. They do not disagree among themselves on the fact that Jesus was the Messiah, the Son of God. Their testimony remained consistent throughout their lives.

Martyred

The final evidence of the truthfulness of the disciples testimony is that they were martyred for their beliefs. The disciples signed their testimony in their own blood. A person might lie for someone else, but will not die for a person or cause if he believes it to be false.

These reasons are sufficient to trust the Gospel portrait of Jesus as given by the New Testament writers.

WHY SHOULD ANYONE BELIEVE MARK AND LUKE SINCE THEY WERE NOT EYEWITNESSES OF THE LIFE OF CHRIST?

Though not eyewitnesses like Matthew and John, Mark and Luke recorded eyewitness testimony. Luke wrote,

> Inasmuch as many have taken in hand to set in order a narrative of those things which are most surely believed among us, just as those who from the beginning were eyewitnesses and ministers of the word delivered them to us, it seemed good to me also, having had perfect understanding of all things from the very first, to write to you an orderly account (Luke 1:1-3).

Luke tells us that he was aware of others who had written about the life of Christ and that he had followed the account from the beginning. Recording the testimony of an eyewitness has the same validity as if that eyewitness had penned the account himself.

The accounts of Mark and Luke do not contradict the eyewitness accounts of Matthew and John. Although independent from the other accounts of the life of Christ, the writers Mark and Luke tell the same basic story. The fact that they themselves were not eyewitnesses is not crucial since the testimony they recorded was from those who witnessed the events.

John Gerstner makes an appropriate observation:

> We note, in the first place, that they had the best possible jury to test their competency—their own contemporaries among whom the events related were said to have taken place. If the writers had been palpably contradicted by the facts, the people to whom they related the facts would have been the very ones to expose them. If they had been misguided zealots the nonzealots to whom they spoke could have spotted in a moment and repudiated it as quickly. If they had garbled the actual events, eyewitnesses in quantity could have testified to the contrary . . . As a matter of fact, their record went unchallenged. No man called them liars; none controverted their story. Those who believed in Jesus did not dispute the claims to his supernatural power. The apostles were imprisoned for speaking about the resurrection of Christ, not, however, on the ground of what they said was untrue, but that it was unsettling the people. They were accused of being heretical, deluded, illegal, un-Jewish, but they were not accused of being inaccurate. And that would have been by far the easiest to prove if it had been thought to be true (John Gerstner, *Reasons For Faith*, Grand Rapids: Baker Book House, 1953, p. 98).

They Were Historically Accurate

It must be emphasized that, as far as we can determine, the Bible is historically accurate. To deny that the miracles occurred would force one to say that the biblical writers were correct when they recorded the names, dates, and places surrounding an event but missed the event itself. It is hard to imagine how writers can get the details correct but miss the main outline.

COULD THE ACCOUNTS OF MIRACLES MERELY BE EXAGGERATIONS?

We have seen that the events, people and places recorded in the Bible demonstrate themselves to be historically accurate. But what about the miracles the Bible records?

The primary reason we accept the miracles of Christ is that they were recorded by eyewitnesses of the events. We have seen how John described his message as,

> That . . . which we have seen with our eyes, which we have looked upon, and our hands have handled, concerning the Word of life (1 John 1:1-3).

Time after time the biblical writers testify that they were eyewitnesses of the miracles they record.

Independent

In the case of the four Gospels, the eyewitnesses to the miracles of Jesus were independent of each other. Although they give the same basic account of the life of Christ, they emphasize different details. Therefore, we have four different writers all testifying that Jesus performed miracles in front of the people.

Surprise Reaction

The reaction to the miracles by believers and unbelievers alike is the same way modern man would react. The people expressed shock and disbelief. Miracles were not the norm. In addition, we are not asked to believe anything out of the ordinary in the area of behavior. Romans acts like Romans, Jews like Jews, men acted like men, and women like women.

Did Not Deny

Another important point is that the unbelievers did not deny the biblical miracles. After witnessing one of the miracles performed by the apostles, the religious rulers commented,

> What should we do to these men? For, indeed, that a notable miracle has been done through them is evident to all who dwell in Jerusalem, and we cannot deny it (Acts 4:16).

Hallucinations?

How do we know that the miracles were were not simply hallucinations? One of the reasons why this theory does not fit the facts is the number of miracles. The miracles performed by Jesus were not infrequent; they were a major part of His ministry.

The Bible says that Jesus' disciples tended to disbelieve reports of the miraculous. When the resurrection was first reported to them they had this response:

> And their words seemed to them as idle tales, and they did not believe them (Luke 24:11).

The disciples were the first unbelievers of the resurrection. The people tended to disbelieve the reports until confronted by the evidence. There was not a mindset for the miraculous.

On the Day of Pentecost Simon Peter said to the crowd:

> Men of Israel, hear these words: Jesus of Nazareth, a Man attested by God to you by miracles, wonders, and signs which God did through Him in your midst, as you yourselves also know (Acts 2:22).

That Simon Peter could appeal to the knowledge of his hearers demonstrates that the miracles of Jesus were an established fact. If they were not, he would have immediately lost his audience. Thus, the idea that the miracles of Jesus were only a result of His disciples' hallucinations does not fit the facts.

In compiling the evidence, there is more than a substantial case that Christ performed the deeds attributed to Him. Since the evidence of Christ miracles is clear and convincing, the burden of proof is upon those who say the events did not occur.

WHAT IS HIGHER CRITICISM?

Higher criticism is the discipline concerned with the authorship of documents. While it is perfectly valid to study the authorship of biblical documents, higher criticism of the Bible has gone far beyond that. Most higher critics seem determined to establish that the Bible is of purely human origin. They deny the very idea that the Bible is the infallible Word of God.

Such denial is not new, of course, for we see it way back in the Garden of Eden, when the serpent said to Eve,

> Has God indeed said, 'You shall not eat of every tree of the garden'? (Genesis 3:1).

The first thing we hear from the mouth of the serpent is the denial of God's Word.

One of the original contentions of higher criticism was that the practice of writing was unknown during the time of Moses; therefore, Moses could not have authored the first five books of the Bible. Sir Frederic Kenyon, the great biblical scholar, wrote:

> About the middle of the nineteenth century there was a period when it was often maintained that writing was unknown in the time of Moses and the Judges and the earlier kings, and consequently that the narratives of these early periods could not be based upon authentic records. This disbelief in the antiquity of writing has been completely disproved by the discoveries of the last

century. First of all, in 1852 and 1853 Henry Layard and his assistant Rassam discovered the libraries of the kings of Assyria at Nineveh, which contained hundreds of tablets of baked clay (the form of book used in Mesopotamia), including the chronicles of Sennacherib, Essarhaddon, and other rulers contemporary with the kings of Israel and Judah. Others contained the Babylonian narratives of the Creation and Deluge. Subsequent discoveries carried back proof of the early use of writing far beyond the time of Moses and even of Abraham (Sir Frederic Kenyon, *The Story of the Bible*, Grand Rapids, Eerdmans, 1967, p. 7).

Thus we see that one of the original contentions of higher critics—that writing did not exist during the early biblical period—has been thoroughly refuted by recent findings. This is but one example of how higher critics refuse to consider in an honest way the Bible's own testimony as to its origin.

Unfair Treatment

Higher criticism claims to treat the Bible as it would any other book. Yet with any other book, good scholarship would demand that we at least consider the book's own statement of who wrote it and why, and that we test it out. In the example we have seen, higher criticism came to faulty conclusions because it insisted that the Bible must be wrong and assumed that Moses—although educated in Pharoah's court, the most advanced environment of his time—couldn't have written the "Books of Moses."

So we conclude that the higher criticism is a valid discipline to a point, studying the authorship of biblical books. But as it has been practiced, it shows a dangerous tendency to reject the idea that the Bible might be what is says it is, God's Word.

WHAT IS FORM CRITICISM?

One of the modern ways in which the Gospels are studied is through the discipline known as form criticism. Form criticism attempts to classify the material found in the Gospels according to their literary form. Such classifications include miracles stories, sayings and narratives. Consequently the Gospels are divided up into different segments known as pericopes and classified accordingly.

While there is nothing wrong with categorizing the Gospels into these different forms, many critics go a step further and attempt to determine the reliability of certain events or sayings according to their form.

Supernatural Jesus

F.F. Bruce points out that form criticism confirms the fact of the supernatural portrait of Jesus as recorded in the New Testament.

> But perhaps the most important result to which Form Criticism points is that, no matter how far back we may press our researches into the roots of the gospel story, no matter how we classify the gospel material, we never arrive at a non-supernatural Jesus . . . All parts of the gospel record are shown by various groupings to be pervaded by a consistent picture of Jesus as Messiah, the Son of God . . . Thus Form Criticism has added its contribution to the overthrow of the hope once fondly

held, that by getting back to the primitive stage of gospel tradition we might recover a purely human Jesus, who simply taught the Fatherhood of God and the brotherhood of man (F.F. Bruce, *The New Testament Documents: Are They Reliable?*, Downers Grove, Ill.: Intervarsity Press, 1979, p. 33).

Problems With Form Critical Approach

While there are some positive features about the form-critical approach, certain problems need to be considered. For one thing, the view of many form critics is that the early church radically changed the events and sayings of Jesus to fit their own needs. The evidence, however does not support this view which is refuted by the following points:

Not Enough Time

The time between the death of Jesus (about A.D. 30) and the first written New Testament document (1 Thessalonians, A.D. 51) is too short for all these supposed changes to occur. Furthermore, the entire New Testament was composed well before the end of the first century with many eyewitnesses to the New Testament events still alive. Any major difference what occurred in the life of Christ and what was recorded would have been easily detected.

Minimize Eyewitness Role

Some form critics maintain that the distortions of the account of the life of Christ took place during His lifetime. But the biblical writers appeal to the fact that they were eyewitnesses of the events they describe. These form critics minimize the role of the eyewitnesses.

No Biographical Interest?

Another argument is that the early church had no biographical interest whatsoever. However, the evidence shows just the opposite. The Gospel accounts are filled with historical details or allusions. Matthew, for example, records Jesus' genealogy (chapter 1), the visit of the Magi to Herod and the slaughter of the innocents (chapter 2), and the events associated with the trial and death of Jesus (chapters 26-27).

In the writings of Luke we also find many historical references. These include:

> Now in the fifteenth year of the reign of Tiberius Caesar, Pontius Pilate being governor of Judea, Herod being tetrarch of Abilene, Annas and Caiaphas being high priests, the word of God came to John the son of Zacharias in the wilderness (Luke 3:1,2).

In this passage seven different people and their governmental positions are listed in order to indicate the time that God's Word came to John the Baptist. The idea that the Gospel writers were not interested in any biographical or historical details of the life of Jesus is not supported by the facts.

Gospels Are Not Folklore

Though many of the form critics would place the Gospels on the same level as folklore, the evidence speaks to the contrary. The life of Jesus, as recorded in the New Testament, is entirely different from folklore. This can be readily seen from other works that attempt to fill in the details of the missing years of the life of Christ. Fanciful stories abound. The miracles recorded in the Bible are always for a specific purpose in the ongoing plan of God and they are accompanied by sufficient eyewitness testimony.

General Outline Forgotten?

It is hard to imagine that the Gospel writers remembered the specific details of the life of Christ but forgot the general outline, as some form critics would have us believe. It is much more plausible to assume that the disciples were correct on the general outline as well as the details.

We conclude that form criticism is a legitimate discipline insofar as it classifies the sayings and deeds of Jesus according to their form without attempting to prove the accuracy of the statements based merely upon the form in which they have been found.

Conclusion on Biblical Criticism

We need to keep several things in mind as we consider the various disciplines known as biblical criticism. C.S.

Lewis, who was intimately familiar with the works of biblical critics, points out the shortcoming of their methods:

> All this sort of criticism attempts to reconstruct the genesis of the text it studies; what vanished documents each author used, when and where he wrote, with what purposes, under what influences . . . This is done with immense erudition and great ingenuity. At first sight it is very convincing . . . What forearms me against all these Reconstructions is the fact that I have seen from the other end of the stick. I have watched reviewers reconstructing the genesis of my own books in just this way . . . My impression is that in the whole of my experience not one of these guesses has on any one point been right; that the method shows a record 100 percent failure . . . Now this surely ought to give us pause. The reconstruction of the history of a text, when the text is ancient, sounds very convincing. But one is after all sailing by dead reckoning; the results cannot be checked by fact. In order to decide how reliable a method is, what more could you ask for than to be shown an instance where the same method is at work and we have the facts to check it by? Well, that is what I have done. And we find, that when this check is available, the results are either always, or nearly always, wrong. The 'assured results of modern scholarship,' as to the way in which an old book was written, are 'assured,' we may conclude because the men who knew the facts are dead and can't blow the gaff (Cited by Walter Hooper, ed., *Christian Reflections*, Grand Rapids, Eerdmans, 1967, n.p.).

Lewis makes several notable points in his essay. Form criticism is not an objective science but a subjective experience based upon the notions of the critic. Form critics are not guided by firm scientific principles. The critics who state their results with great assurance cannot come to any consensus of agreement among themselves. One would think if biblical criticism were such an exact science, as some form critics would have us believe, then they would agree on the results.

Fails Practical Test

The critical approach to Scripture also fails the practical test. If the same critics, who lived at the same time, spoke the same language, and had the same background, still could not reconstruct the circumstances in which Lewis wrote, what makes us think that they can do better when they are dealing with writers of thousands of years ago, writing in a different language with a different culture?

Consequently, where form criticism attempts to answer the question of the historical circumstances in which the biblical writers composed their works, they are found wanting.

CONCLUSION TO PART 3

After looking at the question of the Bible's historical accuracy we can arrive at the following conclusions:

1. The question of the Bible's historical accuracy is of utmost importance because God has revealed Himself through historical events.

2. The New Testament was written soon after the death and resurrection of Christ. There was not enough time for the message to be altered.

3. Those who wrote about Jesus were either eyewitnesses to the events in His life or recorded eyewitness testimony.

4. The New Testament writers encouraged their readers to investigate the historical evidence.

5. There is every reason to trust the testimony of the New Testament writers. They wrote as eyewitnesses, their testimony was consistent, and later they were martyred for their beliefs.

6. Though Scripture has been subjected to various means of criticism, the Bible has demonstrated itself to be a trustworthy historical document. We can, therefore, conclude that the Bible gives an accurate historical portrayal of God intervening in human history.

We now move to Part 4 with questions regarding the inspiration and authority of the Bible. In what sense is the Bible inspired? Does the Bible claim to be infallible? Should we believe everything that it tells us? Did Jesus have anything to say concerning the matter of the Bible's inerrancy? We will examine what the Scripture has to say about these issues.

PART 4

INSPIRATION AND AUTHORITY

WHAT IS REVELATION?

Revelation can be defined as "God's disclosure to human beings of truth they would not otherwise know." The Bible is God's revelation to His intelligent offspring. These truths could not be known through nature, intuition, or any reasoning process.

What Does It Do?

The purpose of revelation is to call humanity into a relationship with God. The Bible says:

> And this is eternal life, that they may know You, the only true God, and Jesus Christ whom You have sent (John 17:3).

To Know Jesus

The Apostle Paul said that his goal was to know Jesus Christ,

> That I may know Him and the power of His resurrection, and the fellowship of His sufferings, being conformed to His death (Philippians 3:10).

Why is it Necessary?

Revelation is necessary because it tells us who God is and what He is like. The Bible says that God,

> alone has immortality, dwelling in unapproachable light, whom no man has seen or can see (1 Timothy 6:16).

God, by nature, is inaccessible to man. Therefore, we can only know as much about Him as He chooses to reveal. Without revelation we are only guessing when we speak about Him.

Divine revelation also reveals God's purpose for mankind. Only by divine revelation can we know who we are and what is the meaning of our existence. Divine revelation informs us that:

1. Man was created in the image of an infinite personal God (Genesis 1:26).

2. Man sinned and became separated from God (Genesis 3:1-24).

3. God became a man in the person of Jesus Christ and bridged the gap between Himself and man by His death on the cross (2 Corinthians 5:21).

4. Each individual is responsible before God and must personally receive Christ as his or her Savior (Romans 6:23).

Without divine revelation we would not know any of these things. Hence, revelation is necessary and reasonable. It is our only basis of speaking meaningfully about God. Without divine revelation all God-talk is meaningless.

Does it Make Sense?

Does it make sense that God would reveal Himself to mankind. The answer is yes. There are several points that need to be made about revelation.

Possible

First, a revelation from God is possible. The Bible says, "with God all things are possible" (Mark 10:27; Luke 1:37). Certainly the all-powerful creator God is able to reveal Himself to His creation if He so desires.

Necessary

A revelation from God is not only possible, it is also necessary. Though sinful man may understand that God does exist, he could not know who God is or what God requires from Him without God specifically revealing Himself. The truths revealed in Scripture can only come through divine revelation. Human opinions and human reasoning are not capable of knowing these things. Truths of God's nature, His plan for mankind can only be known through revelation.

Reasonable

If He has created man with the ability to receive communication it is probable that He do so. If God exists and if His message cannot be known by human intuition or reason then a revelation is probable.

Given the nature of God and man it is reasonable that He would attempt to communicate. It would be strange if He did not contact us.

Certain

Finally we have the certainty of a revelation from God. This is the Bible. The evidence from Scripture shows us that God has spoken.

WHAT IS GENERAL REVELATION?

General revelation, also known as natural revelation, consists of the testimony of God through nature as well as in the conscience of man. Everyone has access to general revelation.

Nature

The Bible speaks of God revealing Himself through nature:

> The heavens declare the glory of God; and the firmament shows His handiwork (Psalm 19:1).

The vastness of the universe gives testimony to God as Creator.

> When I consider Your heavens, the work of Your fingers, the moon and the stars which you have ordained, what is man that you are mindful of him? (Psalm 8:3,4).

God's existence is also made known through His provisions to mankind. Paul urged his hearers to turn to

> the living God who made the heaven, the earth, the sea, and all things that are in them . . . Nevertheless He did not leave Himself without witness, in that He did good, gave us rain from heaven and fruitful seasons, filing our hearts with food and gladness (Acts 14:15-17).

Nature testifies to God's existence. Paul wrote to the church at Rome.

> What may be known of God is manifest in them [all men], for God has shown it to them. For since the creation of the world His invisible attributes are clearly seen, being understood by the things that are made, even His eternal power and Godhead, so that they are without excuse (Romans 1:19,20).

Man's Conscience

The Bible also says that God has revealed Himself to people through their consciences.

> For when Gentiles, who do not have the law, by nature do the things contained in the law, these, although, not having the law, are a law to themselves, who show the work of the law written in their hearts, their conscience also bearing witness, and between themselves their thoughts accusing or else excusing them (Romans 2:14,15).

Because of the evidence from nature and human conscience, everyone is aware of the existence of God. The psalmist wrote:

> The fool has said in his heart, 'There is no God' (Psalm 14:1).

General revelation testifies that God exists, yet it does not tell us any specifics about Him. It is an incomplete foundation for faith, yet prepares each to receive God's special revelation.

WHAT IS SPECIAL REVELATION?

General revelation testifies that God exists. Special revelation, however, reveals the specifics of who God is and what He expects from mankind. The Bible records a variety of ways God has revealed Himself.

Direct Communication

The Bible often records God speaking with an audible voice:

> On the same day the Lord made a covenant with Abram, saying (Genesis 15:18)

> And the Lord God said . . . (Genesis 2:18).

Dreams and Visions

God said to Moses:

> Hear now My words: 'If there is a prophet among you, I, the Lord, make Myself know to him in a vision, and I speak to him in a dream' (Numbers 12:6).

Theophanies

A theophany is the temporary appearance of God in a human body in order to reveal something specific to His people. This has occurred a number of times, according to the Old Testament. The Bible says God appeared in human form to, among others, Abraham, Joshua, and Gideon.

Miracles

A miracle is a sign that points people to God. Miracles reveal the existence and power of God. Peter preached at Pentecost about

> Jesus of Nazareth, a Man attested by God to you by miracles, wonders, and signs which God did through Him in your midst (Acts 2:22).

Prophets

A prophet is a spokesman for God. One such man was Moses, and to him God said,

> Now therefore, go, and I will be with your mouth and teach you what you shall say (Exodus 4:12).

Jesus Christ

God's final word to humanity was through the person of Jesus Christ. Jesus came to earth to reveal God to man.

> God, who at various times and in different ways spoke in time past to the fathers by the prophets, has in these last days spoken to us by His Son (Hebrews 1:1,2).

The Bible

The record of God's direct communication, the theophanies, His miracles, His message to the prophets, and the coming of Jesus Christ is found in the Bible. Hence, mankind need not wonder what God is like or what He expects from us; that information is contained in Scripture.

These are the various ways in which God has revealed Himself.

WHAT IS PROGRESSIVE REVELATION?

The Bible is God's revelation of Himself to man. He did not, however, reveal everything at once. His revelation to man is given in stages, known as progressive revelation.

Old Testament Incomplete

Progressive revelation means that God did not unfold His entire plan to humanity in the Book of Genesis or, for that matter, the whole Old Testament. The Old Testament revelation, though accurate, is incomplete. The fullness of certain teachings cannot be found in the Old Testament. In addition, the Old Testament records predictions that were still to be fulfilled.

Not Less Inspired

Progressive revelation does not mean to purport that the Old Testament is somehow less inspired than the New Testament. It merely states that the revelation found in the New Testament is complete. Jude wrote,

> I found it necessary to write to you exhorting you to contend earnestly for the faith which has once for all delivered to the saints (Jude 3).

The faith has now been once and for all delivered.

Not Contradictory

It is important to understand that progressive revelation does not contradict previous revelations but rather clarifies and develops them. Jesus said the law would be fulfilled, not broken.

> For assuredly, I say to you, till heaven and earth pass away, one jot or tittle will by no means pass from the law till all is fulfilled (Matthew 5:21,22).

Before and After Christ

The Bible makes a distinction between the time before and after Christ.

> For the law was given through Moses, but grace and truth came through Jesus Christ (John 1:17).

> God, who at various times and in different ways spoke in time past to the fathers by the prophets, has in these last days spoken to us by His Son, whom He has appointed heir of all things, through whom also He made the worlds (Hebrews 1:1,2).

Therefore, we see that the Scriptures testify to a progression of God's revelation of Himself to humanity. He did not reveal the fulness of His truth in the beginning, yet what He was revealed was always true.

WHAT IS INSPIRATION?

Though millions of books have been written through the ages, there was only one book written by divine inspiration, the Bible. Inspiration can be defined as the inward working of the Holy Spirit in the lives of men whom God chose to write the books of the Bible. This guaranteed that the final result would be exactly what God intended. Thus, the Bible is the written Word of God to mankind, and, when originally written, was without error. It is the final authority for all matters of faith and practice.

Claims Inspiration

The Bible speaks of itself as being inspired by God. The word *inspiration* is derived from 2 Timothy 3:16.

> All Scripture is given by inspiration of God, and is profitable for reproof, for correction, for instruction in righteousness.

The word translated "inspiration" is the Greek word *theopneustos* meaning "God-breathed."

Elsewhere, the Bible says:

> Knowing this first, that no prophecy of Scripture is of any private interpretation, for prophecy never came by the will of man, but holy men of God spoke as they were moved by the Holy Spirit (2 Peter 1:20,21).

Led by Holy Spirit

The writers of Scripture were led by the Holy Spirit, not their own ideas, in recording the words in the Bible. The resulting text is the Word of God.

Michael Green comments on this verse:

> He [Peter] uses a fascinating maritime metaphor in verse 21 (where the same word, *pheromene*, is used of a ship carried along by the wind). The prophets raised their sails, so to speak (they were obedient and receptive), and the Holy Spirit filled them and carried their craft along in the direction He wished. Men spoke: God spoke (Michael Green *The Second Epistle of Peter and the General Epistle of Jude: An Introduction and Commentary*, London: Tyndale, 1968, p. 91).

The Biblical doctrine of inspiration means that the Bible is God's accurate revelation of Himself. Thus, the Bible cannot be categorized with other literature that causes the human heart to be challenged. It is inspired, nor merely inspiring. It is the Word of God.

Human and Divine

Though all Scripture is God-breathed, it is proper to say that the Bible is a book both human and divine. Its source is God, yet God used human instruments to compose the books.

The Bible is clear that its origin is divine. Jesus made it clear that the Scriptures are the Word of God: He reproved the Pharisees for:

> making the word of God of no effect through your tradition which you have handed down (Mark 7:13).

Here we have the Word of God contrasted with human tradition.

Human Instruments

The Bible, however, is a book which was written through human beings. When one reads the Scriptures, it immediately becomes apparent that the various authors employed different writing styles and different vocabularies giving evidence of their humanity. C.S. Lewis commented upon the human instrumentality:

> The same divine humility which decreed that God should become a baby at a peasant woman's breast, and later an arrested field preacher in the hands of the police, decreed also that he should be preached in a vulgar prosaic and unliterary language. If you can stomach the one, you can stomach the other (C.S. Lewis, Introduction to J.B. Phillips *Letters to Young Churches*, MacMillan 1951).

Therefore, it is proper to say that the inspiration of the Bible has its source in God but that human instruments were used in writing and recording God's Word. This is the biblical teaching on the subject.

IS EVERY STATEMENT OF THE BIBLE TRUE?

When we read the Bible, should we regard every statement as true? Can we confidently read any portion of Scripture and act upon any statement? The answer is no. A distinction needs to be made between the accuracy of the statements in the Bible and truthfulness.

Inspiration guarantees the accuracy of every statement, but not the truth of it. For example, every time Satan spoke, he lied. Jesus said of him,

> He was a murderer from the beginning, and does not stand in the truth, because there is no truth in him. When he speaks a lie, he speaks from his own resources, for he is a liar and the father of it (John 8:44).

In the Garden of Eden the serpent promised Eve that she and her husband would be like God if they ate of the forbidden fruit.

> And the serpent promised Eve that she and her husband would be like God if they ate of the forbidden fruit. And the serpent said to the woman, 'You will not surely die. For God knows in that day you eat of it your eyes will be opened, and you will be like God, knowing good and evil' (Genesis 3:4,5).

The statement of the serpent is recorded accurately, but the statement is not true. Other examples can be found in Scripture where people made statements that are against the clear teaching of God and His Word.

There are also human misstatements in Scripture. The religious leaders said to Nicodemus,

> Are you also from Galilee? Search and look, for no prophet has arisen out of Galilee (John 7:52).

This statement of the religious leaders was not true because the prophet Jonah was from the region of Galilee.

There is also the record of laws that have been done away with. The New Testament says of these laws,

> Therefore let no one judge you in food or in drink, or regarding a festival or a new moon or sabbaths, which are a shadow of things to come, but the substance is of Christ (Colossians 2:16,17).

Each statement of the Bible needs to be read in context. We need to know who is speaking to see whether the statement, though recorded accurately, is in harmony with the truth of God.

WAS THE BIBLE DICTATED BY GOD TO MEN?

Some feel that the authors of the Bible were like stenographers registering the truth of God in the same manner as a tape recorder. They liken it to the claim Muslims make for the Koran, believing that it was dictated by Allah from heaven in the Arabic language.

The idea of a mechanical dictation, though taught by some, is not what the Bible says occurred. It has never been the teaching of the church that the Bible resulted by some sort of dictation from God to the authors.

Different Styles and Personalities

The idea of dictation is easy to refute when one looks at the different biblical books. Each writer has his own personality, style, and vocabulary. For example, the New Testament writings of John are in sharp contrast with those of Luke. John writes a very simple Greek with a limited vocabulary, while Luke writes a much better style of Greek showing greater familiarity with the language.

In addition, the language of the Apostle Paul runs the gamut of emotions. It is hard to reconcile some of the sections where Paul's personality is evident with the idea that he was simply a stenographer.

Use of Sources

The biblical writers also made use of non-biblical sources. The following source books are mentioned in the Old Testament:

* Book of the Wars of the Lord (Numbers 21:14);

* Book of Jasher (Joshua 10:13; 2 Samuel 1:18);

* The records of the Chronicles of King David (1 Chronicles 27:24);

* The Annals on the Book of Kings (2 Chronicles 24:27);

* The Visions of Iddo the Seer (2 Chronicles 9:29; 12:15).

Sometimes the words of the biblical writers resulted from their own careful investigation (Luke 1:1-4). Some would have us believe that there are only two possible ways in which the Bible could have come to man. Either the Bible was dictated by God to man or man alone was involved in the recording of Scripture, resulting in legends, mistakes, and inaccuracies. But neither of these is true. God inspired the biblical writers to use their own personalities, vocabularies, and writing styles to impart His Word to mankind.

HOW DID INSPIRATION OCCUR?

If the Bible was not mechanically dictated by God to man, how did He get His Word through the inspired writers? Scripture does not tell us exactly how the process of inspiration worked. It does, however, tell certain things about the communication of God's truth to man.

Originates With God

The origin of inspiration is in the mind and will of God. The inspiration was given under the direct control of God.

> But we speak the wisdom of God in a mystery, the hidden wisdom which God ordained before the ages for our glory (1 Corinthians 2:7).

Writings Not Writers

According to Scripture it is the writings, the finished product, that are inspired, not the writers themselves. The Bible says the writers were sometimes unaware of the meanings of what they wrote:

> Of this salvation the prophets have inquired and searched diligently, who prophesied of the grace that would come to you, searching what, or what manner of time, the Spirit of Christ who was in them was indicating when He testified beforehand the sufferings of Christ and the glories that would follow (1 Peter 1:10,11).

Daniel did not understand some of the prophecies he recorded.

> Although I heard, I did not understand. Then I said, 'My lord, what shall be the end of these things?' And he said, 'Go your way, Daniel, for the words are closed up and sealed till the time of the end' (Daniel 12:8,9).

Writers in Control

The writers of Scripture wrote under normal circumstances in control of their senses. There are some exceptions to this, where the writers would record dreams or visions granted to them by God, but the usual method was that the writers simply wrote down the truth God wanted revealed. Yet we are at a loss to explain how that happened because the Bible does not tell us. Clark Pinnock comments:

> By confluency is meant the dual authorship of Scripture, the fact that the Bible is at one and the same time the product of the divine breath and a human pen. The miracle of inspiration is analogous to the union in one person of the two natures of Christ; the Word of God in the words of men. This is a mystery that we can only confess and not explain. It is a subject to raise when heaven's school begins its classes, and one about which we dare not claim to know more than we do (Clark Pinnock, *Biblical Revelation*, p. 92).

Though the Bible does not give us exact details of the process of inspiration, it does tell us that the words of Scripture originated with God and were communicated to man in order to produce the resultant Word of God.

DID THE BIBLICAL WRITERS ALWAYS UNDERSTAND THEY WERE RECORDING THE WORD OF GOD?

As we look at the various ways in which inspiration occurred we will find that the writers did not always know that they were recording Holy Scripture.

Understood But Did Not Recognize

Sometimes the writers understood what they were writing, but did not recognize their words as being divine. For example, in his prologue Luke informs us that his work was a result of careful historical investigation (Luke 1:1-4).

Understood and Recognized

The Bible also gives examples where the writers were conscious that they were recording divinely inspired words as well as understanding what they were saying:

> These things we also speak, not in words which man's wisdom teaches but which the Holy Spirit teaches (1 Corinthians 2:13).

Recognized But Did Not Understand

There were other times that the writers did not know the import of their words even though they realized that they were divinely inspired. After receiving prophetic messages from God, the prophet Daniel said, "Although I heard, I did not understand" (Daniel 12:8).

Neither Understood Nor Recognized

In a few instances the statements of Scripture were not understood by those giving them nor were recognized as part of Scripture.

> And one of them, Caiaphas, being high priest that year, said to them, 'You know nothing at all, nor do you consider that it is expedient for us that one man should die for the people, and not that the whole nation should perish.' Now this he did say on his own authority, but being high priest that year he prophesied that Jesus would die for the nation (John 11:49-51).

Inspiration deals with the words, not the men. It is not the people who were inspired, but rather their words were accurately recorded.

WHAT IS THE EVIDENCE THAT THE OLD TESTAMENT IS INSPIRED BY GOD?

Christianity believes and teaches that the Bible, in both the Old and New Testament, has been inspired by God.

Old Testament Claim

First, we must point out that the Old Testament itself claims to be God's Word. The writings were acknowledged as the commandments of the Lord.

> That you may fear the Lord your God to keep all His statues and His commandments which I command you (Deuteronomy 6:2).

These commandments were to be put in the ark of God. The Lord said to Moses,

> And I will write on the tablets the words that were on the first tablets . . . and you shall put them in the ark (Deuteronomy 10:2).

Throughout the entire Old Testament we find references to the writings as coming from God.

The Claim of the New Testament

The New Testament considers the Old Testament to be the Word of God. The Apostle Paul spoke of an authoritative Scripture, referring to the gospel,

> which He promised before through His prophets in the Holy Scriptures (Romans 1:2).

He also saw the Old Testament as predicting justification by faith.

> And the Scripture, foreseeing that God would justify the nations by faith (Galatians 3:8).

Testimony of Jesus

Finally, we have the testimony of Jesus Christ. He made it clear that He believed the Old Testament was God's revelation of Himself to mankind.

Scripture

Jesus recognized the existence of an Old Testament Scripture.

> You search the Scriptures, for in them you think you have eternal life (John 5:39).

Word of God

Jesus said this Old Testament Scripture was the Word of God.

> Why do you transgress the commandment of God because of your tradition? For God commanded, saying, 'Honor your father and your mother' (Matthew 15:3,4).

Unified

He also testified,

> The Scripture could not be broken (John 10:35).

Unalterable

Jesus also made it clear that the Old Testament could not have been altered, even in the slightest,

> For assuredly, I say to you, till heaven and earth pass away, one jot or one tittle will by no means pass from the law till all is fulfilled (Matthew 5:18).

Since Jesus demonstrated Himself to be the Son of God, His word on the matter is final. By definition, God knows everything and Jesus, being God, would know whether or not the Old Testament was His revelation to humanity. He made it clear that it was.

Therefore, we have the witness of the Old Testament, the New Testament, and Jesus Himself that the Old Testament was inspired by God.

WHAT IS THE EVIDENCE THAT THE NEW TESTAMENT IS INSPIRED BY GOD?

The New Testament is considered to be inspired of God for the following reasons:

All throughout Jesus' ministry the divine origin of His words is stressed.

> He who rejects Me, and does not receive My words, has that which judges him—the word that I have spoken will judge him in the last day. For I have not spoken My own authority; but the Father who sent Me gave Me a command, what should I say and what I should speak (John 12:48,49).

In addition, Jesus said His words would never pass away.

> Heaven and earth will pass away, but My words would never pass away (Matthew 24:35).

That Jesus said His words would last forever hints at the idea they would be recorded.

Promise of Jesus

The main reason we believe that the New Testament has been inspired of God is the promise of Jesus. Before

His death and resurrection Jesus made the following promises to His disciples.

> But the Helper, the Holy Spirit, whom the Father will send in My name, He will teach you all things, and bring to your remembrance all things that I said to you (John 14:26).

> But when the Helper comes, whom I shall send to you from the Father, He will testify of Me. And you also will bear witness, because you have been with me from the beginning (John 15:26,27).

> However, when He, the Spirit of truth has come, He will guide you into all truth; for He will not speak on His own authority, but whatever He hears He will speak; and He will tell you things to come (John 16:13).

We have two promises of Jesus contained in these verses:

1. The Holy Spirit would guide these disciples into all truth.

2. They would be given the gift of total recall of the things He said and did.

Anticipates New Testament

These promises look forward to a written body of truth. Those men to whom Jesus made these promises either wrote the books of the New Testament or had control over what writings were considered inspired. Since God had already demonstrated His desire to commit His Word to writing by giving His people the Old Testament, it would follow that He would do the same in a New Testament. The inspiration of the New Testament, therefore, was authenticated ahead of time.

Specific Statements

The New Testament makes specific statements about its inspiration. The Apostle Paul said that his writings were the commandments of the Lord.

> If anyone thinks himself to be a prophet or spiritual, let him acknowledge that the things which I write to you are the commandments of the Lord (1 Corinthians 14:37).

Nothing to be Changed

The disciple John emphasized that no words of Scripture are to be changed.

> For I testify to everyone who hears the words of the prophecy of this book: If anyone adds to these things, God will add to him the plagues that are written in this book; and if anyone takes away from the words of the book of this prophecy, God shall take away his part from the Book of Life (Revelation 22:18,19).

Although the concept of a *completed* New Testament may not be found, we do have the concept of the writings being considered as Scripture. Simon Peter compared the writings of Paul to other Scripture:

> Our beloved brother Paul, according to the wisdom given to him, has written to you, as also in all his epistles . . . which those who are untaught and unstable twist to their own destruction, as they do the rest of Scripture (2 Peter 3:15,16).

Consequently the idea of a written New Testament can be found within the pages of Scripture. The words of the New Testament are equated with the words of God.

WHY ARE THE WRITINGS OF THE APOSTLE PAUL CONSIDERED TO BE INSPIRED?

The Apostle Paul wrote twelve letters that have been recognized as Holy Scripture by the Christian church. What evidence do we have to call Paul's writings Scripture?

Believed His Message to be Divine

The first thing that must be noticed is that Paul believed his message to be divine.

> If anyone thinks himself to be a prophet or spiritual, let him acknowledge that the things which I write to you are the commandments of the Lord (1 Corinthians 14:37).

However, believing to have a divine message does not make it so. What evidence do we have of this message being sent from God.

Paul Received Direct Revelation

The Bible teaches that Paul received direct revelation from God. Paul wrote,

> Have I not seen Jesus Christ our Lord? (1 Corinthians 9:1).

After an encounter with the ascended Jesus on the Damascus road, Paul had it explained by Ananias:

> The God of our fathers has chosen you that you should know His will, and see the Just One, and hear the voice of His mouth. For you will be His witness to all men of what you have seen and heard (Acts 2:14,15).

Were Considered Scripture During His Lifetime

The final point is that the New Testament recognized Paul's writing as Scripture. Peter wrote:

> Our beloved brother Paul, according to the wisdom given to him, has written to you, as also in all his epistles, speaking in them of these things, in which some things are hard to understand, which those who are untaught and unstable twist to their own destruction, as they do the rest of the Scriptures (2 Peter 3:15,16).

The writings of Paul complete the New Testament. He was the chosen instrument to explain the meaning of the two comings of Jesus Christ.

TO WHAT EXTENT IS THE BIBLE INSPIRED?

The terms used to describe the inspiration of the Bible is *verbal plenary*. When we speak of *verbal* inspiration we mean that every word has been inspired by God. This means the very words were chosen by God. *Plenary* inspiration means fully, in all parts. The Bible in all parts is inspired by God. The evidence for verbal plenary inspiration can be found in Scripture.

Importance of Every Word

The Bible testifies to the importance of every word. Sometimes an important truth hinges on the use of a certain word or group of words. For example, the Apostle Paul argued from the use of a word in the singular rather than in the plural.

> Now to Abraham and his Seed were the promises made. He does not say, 'And to seeds,' as of many, but as of one, 'And to your Seed,' who is Christ (Galatians 3:16).

All Parts Inspired

The Scripture teaches that all parts are inspired by God.

> All Scripture is given by inspiration of God, and is profitable for doctrine, for reproof, for correction, for instruction in righteousness (2 Timothy 3:16).

The Apostle Paul wrote to the church at Rome,

> For whatever things were written before were written for our learning, that we through patience and comfort of the Scriptures might have hope (Romans 15:4).

Paul says the former writings, the Old Testament, were written for our instruction. He does not exclude anything from the Old Testament but rather includes everything. There is no distinction between some parts of Scripture that are true and others that are not. All of the writings are assumed to be true.

We conclude therefore, that every word of the sixty-six books of the Bible is inspired by God. This means that the final record of Scripture says exactly what God wanted it to say.

WHAT IS INERRANCY?

One of the terms used in describing the Bible is inerrancy. Though inerrancy is a new term (coined within the last one hundred years), it describes a true concept.

Inerrancy, or infallibility, means that when all the facts are known the Bible, in the original autographs, will prove itself to be without error in all matters that it covers, including theology, history, science, and all other disciplines of knowledge. The biblical doctrine of inerrancy is understood with the following qualifications.

Original Documents

Inerrancy only covers the original writings of the authors of Scripture. There is no claim that the various copies of the manuscripts made throughout the years are inerrant.

Inerrancy extends to the writings of the different authors, not the writers themselves. The finished product is error-free, not the men who wrote the documents.

Non-scientific Descriptions

The doctrine of inerrancy allows for the Bible to be written in non-technical descriptions. We must allow for a biblical writer to explain a natural event from the point of view of an observer (e.g. "the sun goes down"). We do not need to assume the writer is making a scientific statement about the nature of the universe when such a statement is made.

Allows Different Details

The doctrine of inerrancy also allows for different writers to describe the same events with different details. The Gospels record many of the same events with explanations that do not match word for word. These explanations are not contradictory, they merely emphasize different details.

Allows Pictorial Language

Holding to an inerrant Bible allows for pictorial language and figures of speech. Interpreting the Bible literally does not rule out figurative language when the context calls for it. The Bible uses literary devices such as metaphor, simile, and hyperbole to make a point. Truth can be communicated through figures of speech.

Not Strict Rules of Grammar

The doctrine of inerrancy does not demand the adherence to the rules of grammar. There are examples of biblical writers breaking the strict rules of grammar to emphasize certain points. The Book of Revelation, for instance, is filled with some examples. Many ancient as well as modern writers employ this technique to emphasize a point. The writers of Scripture should not be denied this literary usage.

DOES THE BIBLE TESTIFY TO ITS OWN INERRANCY?

Yes. The authors of Scripture make it clear that they are recording the Word of God. The people were told not to add to or subtract from that which God commanded.

> You shall not add to the word which I command you (Deuteronomy 4:2).

Paul wrote to the Thessalonians,

> For this reason we also thank God without ceasing, because when you received the word of God which you heard from us, you welcomed it not as the word of men, but as it is in truth, the word of God (1 Thessalonians 2:13).

Word of God Always True

The Bible also testifies that the Word of God is always true.

> I, the Lord, speak righteousness, I declare the things that are right (Isaiah 45:19).

> Every word of God is pure . . . Do not add to His words, lest He reprove you, and you be found a liar (Proverbs 30:5,6).

Thus we find two concepts in the Scripture regarding its nature. First, it is clearly the Word of God, and second, it is always true. There is never a hint that errors can be found in any part of Scripture. John Wesley, the founder of the Methodist church, wrote,

> If there be any mistakes in the Bible, there may well as be a thousand. If there be one falsehood in that book, it did not come from the God of truth (John Wesley Journal, Wednesday July 24, 1776).

The only consistent position is to believe the Bible is without error; this is the position of the Bible itself. However believing in an inerrant Bible is not necessary for salvation.

HAS THE CHURCH HISTORICALLY TAUGHT THAT THE BIBLE IS INERRANT?

It is clear from the writings of the early Christians that they held to an inerrant Scripture. Theologian George Duncan Barry, who himself rejected the biblical doctrine of inerrancy, made it clear that the church has always held to an inerrant Bible:

> The fact that for fifteen centuries no attempt was made to formulate a definition of the doctrine of inspiration of the Bible, testifies to the universal belief of the Church that the Scriptures were the handiwork of the Holy Ghost . . . it ruled out all possibility of error in matters either of history or of doctrine. Men expressed their belief in the inspiration and authority of the Bible in language which startles us by its strange want of reserve. The Scriptures were regarded as writings of the Holy Spirit, no room at all being left for the play of the human agent in the Divine Hands. The writers were used by Him as a workman uses his tools; in a word, the Books, the actual words, rather than the writers, were inspired (George Duncan Barry, *The Inspiration and Authority of Holy Scripture,* A Study of the First Five Centuries, New York: Macmillan, 1919, p. 10).

Barry's statement is highly instructive, for it reveals that some of those who reject the doctrine of inerrancy realize that the church has universally held to it. Furthermore, it indicates that the very words of Scripture, from beginning to end, were assumed to be inspired by God.

Recent Developments

Though the church has throughout its history believed the Bible to be inerrant, recent developments have moved away from this position. An example can be seen in the Roman Catholic view of Scripture. In 1907 the Catholic Encyclopedia has this to say concerning the Bible:

> The Bible . . . is the word of God . . . The inerrancy of the Bible follows as a consequence of Divine authorship. Wherever the sacred writer makes a statement as his own, the statement is the word of God and infallibly true, whatever the subject matter of the statement (*The Catholic Encyclopedia*, Robert Appleton, ed., vol. 2, 543).

This is the historic view of the church as a whole. However, one of the latest volumes of the Catholic Encyclopedia takes a different view.

> The inerrancy of Scripture has been the constant teaching of the Fathers, the theologians, and recent Popes in the encyclicals on Biblical studies . . . It is nonetheless obvious that many biblical statements are simply not true when judged according to modern knowledge of science and history (New Catholic Encyclopedia, Vol. 2, New York: McGraw-Hill, 1967, p. 384).

Though the term inerrancy is relatively new, coined in the last one hundred years, the teaching of inerrancy is not. We conclude that the doctrine of inerrancy was taught and believed universally by the church up until modern times, when some have denied its truth.

IS THE DOCTRINE OF INERRANCY IMPORTANT?

Some argue that the doctrine of inerrancy is not important, that the key issue is a person's relationship to Jesus Christ, not the nature of the Bible. But those who advocate an errant Scripture have seriously undermined the Bible's authority.

If a person denies the doctrine of inerrancy, in effect, he is denying God's Word. The Old Testament scholar Edward Young wrote,

> He, of course tells us His Word is pure. If there are any mistakes in that Word, however, we know better; it is not pure . . . He declares that His law is truth, His law contains the truth, let us grant Him that, but we know that it contains error. If the autographs of Scripture are marred by flecks of mistake, God simply has not told us the truth concerning His Word. To assume that He could breathe forth a Word that contained mistakes is to say, in effect, that God Himself can make mistakes (E. J. Young, *Thy Word Is Truth*, Grand Rapids: Eerdmans, 1957, p. 87).

Without a Word from God we are left without a firm foundation. Each individual would be the final determiner as to what is God's truth and what is not. The Christian faith would be built upon sand, not upon the solid foundation of God's Word.

We conclude the doctrine of inerrancy is of the utmost importance.

DOES INERRANCY EXTEND TO ALL MATTERS SCIENTIFIC AND HISTORICAL?

Does inerrancy extend to all matters scientific and historical? Some people do not believe so. They teach that a person can accept the biblical teaching about God, heaven, hell, salvation, etc. without accepting the statements the Bible makes concerning historical or scientific matters. This view is known variously as "revelational inerrancy," "dynamic inspiration," or "limited inerrancy."

Is this an option? George Ladd writes,

> If the Bible is the sure Word of God, does it follow that we must have a trustworthy word from God, not only in matters of faith and practice, but in all historical and factual questions? 'Thus saith the Lord' means that God has spoken in His sure, infallible Word. A corollary of this in the minds of many Christians is that we must have absolute, infallible answers to every question raised in the historical study of the Bible. From this perspective, the 'critic' is the one who has surrendered the Word of God for the words of men, authority for speculation, certainty for uncertainty. The conclusion, as logical and persuasive as it may seem, does not square with the facts of God's Word; and it is the author's hope that the authority of the Word of God is not dependent upon infallible certainty of all matters of history and criticism (George E. Ladd, *The New Testament and Criticism*, Grand Rapids, Eerdmans, 1967, p. 16).

According to Ladd, as well as many others, it is proper to make the distinction between the theological and historical statements. But the Bible makes no such distinction. On the contrary, the Bible teaches that all Scripture is inspired of God:

> All Scripture is given by inspiration of God, and is profitable for doctrine, reproof, for correction, for instruction in righteousness, that the man of God may be complete, thoroughly equipped for every good work (2 Timothy 3:16).

No Basis of Authority

If the biblical writers were mistaken in their historical, geographical and scientific references then why, one might ask, should their statements in the theological realm be trusted? It is meaningless to assert that the biblical writers made errors in history, science, and geography, but were kept error-free when they recorded statements in the theological realm (heaven, hell, salvation, etc.). We may rightly ask, "In what sense is the Bible inspired?"

Reversing Roles

The problem with this point of view is to determine exactly which statements are inspired and which are not. The questions which immediately arise are these: Who decides what is true? How can one differentiate between facts and teaching? How can one separate the essential message of the teaching of the Bible from the background in which it is presented? There is certainly no such distinction recognized in Scripture itself. The whole Bible comes to us and offers itself to us exactly the same way, giving us no reason to suspect that parts of it are inspired and parts are not. Whoever does this sets himself above the Bible and reverses roles with God.

Lawyer/theologian John Warwick Montgomery offers this helpful comment:

> Christ's attitude toward the Old Testament was one of total trust: nowhere, in no particular, and on no subject did he place Scripture under criticism. Never did he distinguish truth in 'faith in practice' from veracity in historical and secular matters, and he told the Evil Foe in no uncertain terms that man lives 'by every word that proceedeth out of the mouth of God' (Matt. 4:4 quoting Deut. 8:3). To his apostles, under whose scrutiny the New

> Testament was written, he promised His Holy Spirit, who 'shall bring all things to your remembrance, whatsoever I have said to you' (John 14:26; cf. 2 Peter 3:15,16). (John Warwick Montgomery, *Christianity Today*, March 3, 1967, p. 48).

Inerrant in All Matters

There is no hint that any of the biblical statements, whether historical or theological, should be questioned. To make such a distinction is neither needful nor helpful.

We conclude that the inerrancy of Scripture does extend to all matters scientific and historic.

WHAT OBJECTIONS HAVE BEEN MADE AGAINST INERRANCY?

The doctrine of inerrancy has been met with objection from within and without the Christian community. The objections include the following:

Bible Does Not Clearly Teach Inerrancy

Though the Bible does not use the word *inerrancy* in describing itself, the teaching of inerrancy is contained within Scripture. The Scripture claims to be the Word of God and the Word of God is always true. The logical conclusion to this is that the Bible is without error.

Human Nature

One objection that always comes up against inerrancy of the Bible is human nature. It is the nature of human beings to make mistakes and, since the Bible was written by men, we should expect it to contain mistakes. Yet this overlooks the fact that, although men do make mistakes, they do not have to make mistakes. Furthermore, this line of reasoning would lead to the idea that Adam and Eve were not human until they made mistakes. It is not impossible, given the nature of man, that the Bible could have written in an error-free manner.

In addition, the Bible itself testifies that it is without error because God providentially inspired the writers to record exactly what He wanted to be recorded. Therefore, the appeal to mistake-prone human nature in not a valid objection against inerrancy. Humans can perform error-free acts.

Mistakes in Copies

The mistakes in the different copies of the biblical manuscripts have also been used as an argument against inerrancy. The solution to this question is simple. Copies are not the same as the original. Furthermore, as we get closer in time to the originals, the number of copyists' errors in the manuscripts decreases. In addition, the manuscript variations do not materially affect the meaning of the text. Inerrancy is not affected by errors in copies written from the original.

Modern Science

Modern science has supposedly rendered an inerrant Bible as an impossibility. Reports of skulls of creatures who were half-man, half-ape, assumptions that the earth is billions of years old, as well as confident assertions that the theory of evolution has been proved have led many to abandon the idea of an inerrant Bible. Yet none of these assertions have come anywhere near to "scientific certainty." Furthermore, we need to have a proper understanding of what the Bible actually says and does not say about science (For further reading see Don Stewart, *What The Bible Says About Science,* Orange, California, Dart Press, 1992).

Modern Biblical Scholarship:

Some have felt that modern biblical scholarship has demonstrated that it is no longer possible to hold to an inerrant Scripture. But this is not the case. Discoveries in the last century have done much to vindicate the Bible's trustworthiness. *Time* magazine conceded that fact:

> After more than two centuries of facing the heaviest scientific guns that could be brought to bear, the Bible has survived—and is perhaps better for the siege. Even on the critics' own terms—historical fact—the Scriptures seem more acceptable now than they did when the rationalists began the attack (*Time*, December 30, 1974).

Old Testament Citations

If the Scripture teaches inerrancy, why didn't the New Testament writers cite the Old Testament writers word for word? The lack of verbal exactness in citing the Old Testament has caused some to deny the biblical teaching of inerrancy. One thing to remember is that the Old Testament was written in Hebrew while the New Testament was composed in Greek. The quote, therefore, cannot be given word for word because you are dealing with two different languages.

Another thing that needs to be emphasized is that the ancients did not use the same type of punctuation as we do today. There were no punctuation marks, ellipses, brackets, or other such devices. Consequently, we do not know whether the ancient writer was citing something directly or alluding to it.

Worship of the Bible

Some have argued that the doctrine of inerrancy makes one worship the Bible rather than God. It creates a paper pope. But this is not the case. The believer puts his faith in the God of the Bible based upon what the infallible Word says.

Missing Autographs

How can the Christian church assert the Bible is inerrant if it does not have have the original writings?

We do not have to appeal to the lost original manuscripts in order to hold the doctrine of inerrancy. The number of places where there are scribal discrepancies in the text are few, and have plausible solutions. It is not the case that the Christian has to continually appeal to some "lost original" to solve the problems of an inerrant Scripture.

Though we have not seen inerrant originals we have not seen errant ones either. In addition, the church has never seen the risen Christ but still believes in Him. Simon Peter wrote of Jesus Christ:

> Whom having not seen you love. Though now you do not see Him, yet believing you rejoice (1 Peter 1:7,8).

We love Jesus and believe Him to be the Savior based upon the best evidence. The same holds true for an inerrant Bible. We base our belief not on blind faith but upon the weight of the evidence. The idea that we cannot see an inerrant autograph should not destroy our faith in one.

The objections raised against inerrancy, therefore, do not weaken the case for its truth. Believing the Bible to be inerrant is the consistent Christian position.

DID JESUS BELIEVE THE SCRIPTURES WERE WITHOUT ERROR?

When we examine the way Jesus viewed Scripture we can see that He trusted it totally. He said the Word of God was true:

> Sanctify them by Your truth. Your word is truth (John 17:17).

Jesus also said the Scripture could not be broken (John 10:35).

It is clear from Jesus' statements that He believed the Bible to be without error. Even scholars who do not believe that the Bible is inerrant realize that this was the belief of Jesus. Kenneth Kantzer writes of these people,

> H. J. Cadbury, Harvard professor and one of the more extreme New Testament critics of the last generation once declared he was far more sure as an historical fact that Jesus held to the common Jewish belief of an infallible Bible than that Jesus believed in His own Messiahship. Adolph Harnack, greatest church historian of modern times, insists that Christ was one with His apostles, the Jews, and the entire early Church, in complete commitment to the infallible authority of the Bible. John Knox, author of what is perhaps the most highly regarded recent life of Christ, states that there can be no question that this view of the Bible was taught by

the Lord Himself (Harold Lindsell, ed., *The Church's Worldwide Mission*, Waco, Texas: Word, 1966, p. 31).

Therefore, it is clear that Jesus accepted the view that the Old Testament was without error.

Since Jesus demonstrated total trust in the Scriptures, we have three different ways in which we can look at the matter.

Deceiver

If Jesus knew the Scriptures contained errors but taught the people that they were error-free, then He was a deceiver. This would make Jesus guilty of lying. Whatever His motive may have been, it would prove that we can neither trust Him nor the Scriptures.

Ignorant

If the Bible contains factual errors of which Jesus did not know, then it affects the way we view Him. If He were ignorant of this fact, then it is possible that He was ignorant of other facts. John Warwick Montgomery writes,

> Logically if the Bible is not inerrant and Jesus thought it was, He can hardly be the incarnate God He claimed to be and for whom the same claims are made by His Apostles. Had He been mistaken on this point, the church could well ask whether any single teaching of Jesus on any subject (including the way of salvation) might not also reflect His sincere misunderstanding. A 'God' of this kind (even if He were indeed divine) would do us no more good than a non-God, for in neither case could we confidently rely upon His teachings (John Warwick Montgomery, *God's Inerrant Word*, Bethany House Publishers, 1974, p. 29).

The Bible is Inerrant

The only alternative that fits the facts is that Jesus taught the inerrancy of the Bible because He knew it was true.

Thus, if we are to be consistent we will approach the Bible in the same manner as our Lord—believing it to be error-free.

CONCLUSION TO PART 4

After examining the subject of the Bible's inspiration and authority we can make the following conclusion:

1. The Bible says that God has revealed Himself to mankind by various means.

2. According to Scripture, it is absolutely necessary that God reveal Himself to us.

3. Apart from Divine revelation, we would not know any of the truths of the Bible.

4. The Bible claims to be God's inspired Word.

5. Though God used human instruments, the words of Scripture conveyed exactly what God wanted to say.

6. Because the Bible says exactly what God wanted to communicate, it is inerrant in every matter it speaks about.

7. Jesus testified to the Bible's inerrancy. If He is Whom He claimed to be, God the Son, then His Word is final.

In our next section we will consider the question of the canon. Are the correct books in the Bible? Has any book been left out that should be there? What about modern works that claim biblical authority? Can any new book be added to the Bible today?

PART 5

THE CANON

WHAT IS THE CANON OF SCRIPTURE?

One of the terms used in describing the books that belong in Scripture is the word canon. This comes from the Greek word *kanon*, meaning reed or measurement. A canonical book is one that measures up to the standard of Holy Scripture. Thus, the canon of Scripture refers to the books that are considered the authoritative Word of God.

Old Testament Canon

The idea of a finished Old Testament canon was spoken by both biblical and nonbiblical sources. Flavius Josephus, a Jewish writer of the first century, had this to say:

> We have but twenty-two [books] containing the history of all time, books that are justly believed in; and of these, five are the books of Moses, which comprise the law and earliest traditions from the creation of mankind down to his death. From the death of Moses to the reign of Artaxerxes, King of Persia, the successor of Xerxes, the prophets who succeeded Moses wrote the history of the events that occurred in their own time, in thirteen books. The remaining four documents comprise hymns to God and practical precepts to men (William Whiston, trans., Flavius Josephus against Apion, Vol. I, in *Josephus, Complete Works*, Grand Rapids, Kregel, 1960, p. 8).

Biblical scholar Gleason Archer comments on the impact of the statement made by Josephus:

> Note three important features of this statement: (1) Josephus includes the same three divisions of the Hebrew Scriptures as does the MT [Massoretic text] (although restricting the third group to 'hymns' and *hokhmah*), and he limits the number of canonical books in these three divisions to twenty-two. (2) No more canonical writings have been composed since the reign of Artaxerxes, son of Xerxes (464-424 B.C.), that is, since the time of Malachi. (3) No additional material was ever included in the canonical twenty-two books during the centuries between (i.e., from 425 B.C. to A.D. 90). Rationalist higher critics emphatically deny the last two points, but they have to do with the witness of such an early author as Josephus and explain how the knowledge of the allegedly post-Malachi date of sizable portions, such as Daniel, Ecclesiastes, Song of Solomon, and many of the psalms, had been kept from this learned Jew in the first century A.D. It is true that Josephus also alludes to apocryphal material (as from 1 Esdras and 1 Maccabees); but in view of the statement quoted above, it is plain that he was using it merely a historical source, not as divinely inspired books (Gleason Archer Jr., *A Survey of Old Testament Introduction,* Revised Edition, Chicago: Moody Press, 1974, p. 71).

Josephus also declared:

> And how firmly we have given credit to those books of our own nation is evident by what we do; for during so many ages as have already passed, no one has been so bold as either to add anything to them or take anything from them, or to make any change in them; but it becomes natural to all Jews, immediately and from their very birth, to esteem those books to contain divine doctrines, and to persist in them, and, if occasion be, willing to die for them. For it is no new thing for our captives, many of them in numbers, and frequently in time, to be seen to endure racks and deaths of all kinds upon the theatres, that they may not be obliged to say one word against our laws, and the records that contain them (Josephus, Ibid., p. 609).

New Testament

The biblical evidence also testifies to a completed Old Testament. From the Gospels we see that Jesus spoke of Scripture as being complete. He said to the religious rulers:

> You search the Scriptures, for in them you think you have eternal life (John 5:39).

> These are the words which I spoke to you while I was still with you, that all things must be fulfilled which were written in the Law of Moses and the Prophets and the Psalms concerning Me (Luke 24:44).

The law, the writings, and the prophets were the threefold division of Old Testament Scripture. Jesus testified to their authenticity.

New Testament Canon

Although the New Testament does not speak of a completed canon of Scripture, it does testify to writings already considered to be the Word of God. Peter recognized the writings of the Apostle Paul as Scripture. He cited Paul's letters, which some were twisting "as they do the rest of the Scriptures" (2 Peter 3:15,16).

When Paul wrote to Timothy he quoted a passage from Luke as Scripture.

> For the Scripture says, 'You shall not muzzle an ox while it treads the grain,' and, 'the laborer is worthy of his wages' (1 Timothy 5:18).

The first verse quoted is from Deuteronomy, but the second is a quotation of one of our Lord's statements recorded by Luke: "The laborer is worthy of his wages" (Luke 10:7).

Formation

The formation of the New Testament canon began in the early part of the second century A.D. The earliest list was drawn up in Rome, in A.D. 140, by the heretic Marcion. Although his list was not authoritative, it did demonstrate that the idea of a New Testament canon was accepted at that time.

The concept we have today of a completed Bible was formulated early in the history of the church. By the end of the second century all but seven books (Hebrews, 2 and 3 John, 2 Peter, Jude, James, and Revelation) were recognized as apostolic, and by the end of the fourth century all twenty-seven books in our present canon were recognized by all the churches of the West.

After the Damasine Council of Rome in A.D. 332 and the third Council of Carthage in A.D. 397 the question of the canon was closed in the West. By the year 500 the whole Greek-speaking church had also accepted all the books in our present New Testament.

WHO DECIDED WHICH BOOKS SHOULD BE PLACED IN THE BIBLE?

Many people wonder who decided which books should be placed in the Bible.

The simple answer is that God decided which books should be in the canon. He was the final determiner. J. I. Packer writes:

> The church no more gave us the New Testament canon than Sir Isaac Newton gave us the force of gravity. God gave us gravity, by his work of creation, and similarly he gave us the New Testament canon, by inspiring the individual books that make it up (J. I. Packer, *God Speaks To Man*, p. 81).

Canonizing and Collecting

A distinction needs to be made between canonizing and collecting. No man or council can pronounce a work canonical or scriptural, yet man was responsible for collecting and preserving such works. F. F. Bruce writes:

> One thing must be emphatically stated. The New Testament books did not become authoritative for the Church because they were formally included in a canonical list; on the contrary, the Church included them in her canon because she already regarded them as divinely inspired, recognizing their innate worth and

> generally apostolic authority, direct or indirect. The first ecclesiastical councils to classify the canonical books were both held in North Africa—at Hippo Regius in 393 and at Carthage in 397—but what these councils did was not to impose something new upon the Christian communities but to codify what was already the general practice of these communities (F. F. Bruce, *The New Testament Documents: Are They Reliable?*, Grand Rapids, Eerdmans, 1960, p. 27).

Hence the books we have as Scripture were inspired by God and recognized such by man.

WHAT CRITERIA WERE USED IN DETERMINING WHICH BOOKS BELONGED IN THE BIBLE?

The books admitted to the canon of Scripture were inspired by God. There were, however, many false books that claimed inspiration. How did the people judge between the true and the false? The Bible does not give any set of criteria that were used to determine which books were to be considered Scripture. We are not told how the determination was made. Though we do not know the exact criteria which were used, they may include the following:

Prophetic Authorship

For a book to be considered canonical, it must have been written by a prophet or apostle or by one who had a special relationship to such (Mark to Peter, Luke to Paul). Only those who had witnessed the events or had recorded eyewitness testimony could have their writings considered as Holy Scripture.

Witness of the Spirit

The appeal to the inner witness of the Holy Spirit was also made to aid the people in understanding which books belonged in the canon and which did not. Clark Pinnock writes:

> The Spirit did not reveal a list of inspired books, but left their recognition to a historical process in which He was active. God's people learned to distinguish wheat from chaff, and gold from gravel, as He worked in their hearts (Clark Pinnock, *Biblical Revelation*, Grand Rapids: Baker Book House, 1973, p. 104).

Acceptance

The final test is the acceptance of the people of God. Jesus told His disciples:

> But the Helper, the Holy Spirit, whom the Father will send in My name, He will teach you all things, and bring to your remembrance all things which I said to you (John 14:26).

We have the promise of Jesus that His disciples would be given total recall by the Holy Spirit of the things He said and did. These same disciples either wrote the New Testament books or had input into which works were accepted as Scripture. Any book that claimed canonical status, yet diverted from the truth of the life of Christ, would have been rejected by Jesus' own disciples who were eyewitnesses to the New Testament events. Thus, the acceptance of God's people is an important criterion for a book to be considered canonical.

HOW DO WE KNOW THE CORRECT BOOKS ARE IN THE BIBLE?

The Bible, as we have it today, consists of sixty-six books. The fact that these books belong as Holy Scripture is confirmed by the testimony of Jesus Christ.

First, with regard to the Old Testament we have the testimony of Jesus to the existing books. He confirmed the accepted three-fold division of our canonical books.

> These are the words which I spoke to you while I was still with you, that all things must be fulfilled which were written in the Law of Moses and the Prophets and the Psalms concerning Me (Luke 24:44).

The Promise of Jesus

As far as the New Testament is concerned, we have the promise of Jesus.

> But the Helper, the Holy Spirit, whom the Father will send in My name, He will teach you all things, and bring to your remembrance all things that I said to you (John 14:26).

Though we do not have His guarantee after the fact, we have this promise that a New Testament would be given. Thus, we have Jesus "pre-authenticating" the New Testament.

Nature of God

Another reason we can be assured the correct books are in the Bible is the nature of God. It has been estimated there are a quintillion stars in the universe and the Bible says God calls them by their names. If God is able to do this, He certainly is able to preserve intact His Word for the benefit of mankind.

Conclusion

Since we have the testimony of Jesus that God preserved the Old Testament for His people, we can also be assured that God took the same care in preserving the New Testament books. When the evidence is examined, we find it consistent and credible.

DO JEWS AND CHRISTIANS USE THE SAME OLD TESTAMENT?

The Old Testament consists of thirty-nine books according to the Protestant reckoning but only twenty-four according to the Jewish reckoning. The books are the same; the difference is in the way they are divided.

Protestant Bible

The division of the Protestants' Bible is as follows: seventeen historical books: Genesis—Esther: five poetical books Job-Song of Solomon: seventeen prophetical books: Isaiah—Malachi.

Hebrew Division

The Hebrew Bible numbers these as twenty-four: The Torah or law contains five books, Genesis—Deuteronomy; The Prophets contain eight books, Joshua, Judges, Samuel, Kings, Isaiah, Jeremiah, Ezekiel, and the twelve minor prophets are grouped into one book; The Writings or *Kethubim* contain eleven books, Psalms, Proverbs, Song of Solomon, Ruth, Lamentations, Ecclesiastes, Esther, Daniel, Ezra—Nehemiah, and Chronicles.

The Hebrew Bible combined 1 and 2 Samuel, 1 and 2 Kings, and 1 and 2 Chronicles. The twelve minor prophets were combined into one book. Josephus numbered the books as twenty-two by attaching Ruth to Judges and Lamentations to Jeremiah.

Thus, the books are identical. The only difference is in the way they are divided.

WHAT EFFECT DID THE COUNCIL OF NICEA HAVE ON DETERMINING WHAT BOOKS BELONGED IN THE BIBLE?

There have been accusations that the council of Nicea had a tremendous effect on both choosing what books should be in the Bible and changing some of the doctrines that the church held before that time.

The council of Nicea met in A.D. 323 to discuss how Jesus Christ was related to God. There were some in the church, led by Arius of Alexandria, who denied that Jesus Christ was God in human flesh, the Second Person of the Trinity. In order to answer these issues, the church had to make a pronouncement about which books authoritative doctrine could be based on.

The council of Nicea did not meet to discuss which books belonged in the New Testament canon. It only recognized the books that the church had from the beginning considered to be the Word of God.

Already Composed

The books that were recognized as Scripture had already been composed at the time. All the books contained in the New Testament were composed before the end of the first century. Some fifty existing papyrus manuscripts written before A.D. 325 contain parts of every book of the New Testament except 1 Timothy.

There is no truth to the argument, so often brought up, that some of these books were not in existence until the council of Nicea. The argument, therefore, that certain doctrines were invented at this time has no basis in fact.

SHOULD OTHER EARLY WRITINGS BE PLACED IN THE BIBLE?

There are some very early works in the history of the church that add to our information about Jesus. These books written between A.D. 80 and A.D. 180, were composed by "apostolic fathers." Although they were not inspired, as the New Testament books are, they do provide us with some confirming information regarding the New Testament events. Some of the most notable examples include:

Letter of Clement

In A.D. 95 Clement of Rome wrote a letter to the Corinthian church. This is an extremely important work because Clement was the leading elder of the church of Rome. He wrote his letter to the Corinthians to end a dispute between the laity and the elders.

Ignatius of Antioch

Ignatius of Antioch wrote seven letters in A.D. 115 on his way to being thrown to the lions. He made the distinction between his writings and that of the apostles.

> I do not enjoin you as Peter and Paul did. They were apostles, I am a convict; they were free, but I am a slave to this very hour (Ignatius, *Letter to the Romans*, 4.3).

Quadratus

Quadratus was one of the earliest defenders of the Christian faith. He wrote to the Emperor Hadrian about A.D. 125. The work has been lost except for a brief statement in the writing of the church historian Eusebius.

> The deeds of our saviour were always before you, for they were true miracles; those who were healed, those who were raised from the dead, who were seen, not only were healed and when raised but were always present. They remained living a long time, not only whilst our Lord was on earth, but likewise when he left the earth. So that some of them have also lived to our own times.

Quadratus gives another account of the miracles of Jesus and testifies as the Apostle Paul does that many who participated in the miraculous events surrounding the life of Christ lived long after Jesus ascended into heaven.

The Epistle of Barnabas

The Epistle of Barnabas, not the Barnabas of the New Testament, was written between A.D. 130 and 138. It was written to show that Jesus is a fulfillment of the Old Testament law.

Though these books were written at an early date, they have never been seriously considered as Holy Scripture. They do not claim biblical authority, some actually disclaim it. In addition, none of them were written by apostles or members of the apostolic company. But they are helpful in shedding light on the New Testament.

WHY WAS THE AUTHORITY OF CERTAIN OLD TESTAMENT BOOKS QUESTIONED?

At certain times some of the biblical books had their authority questioned. These include:

Esther

The problem with the Book of Esther is that the name of God is not found in the book. The hand of God, however, is certainly evident in the story as He protected the Jews from total annihilation. The mere absence of God's name is not sufficient reason to deny its status, especially when His providential hand is so evident.

Ecclesiastes

Ecclesiastes was sometimes objected to because of its skeptical tone. The writer of the book exclaims, "Vanity of vanity, all is vanity" (Ecclesiastes 1:2). The problem here is a matter of understanding the author's intent. Solomon, the writer of the book, is demonstrating that no one can experience ultimate satisfaction in this world. He shows that all people need God.

Song of Solomon

The Song of Solomon was sometimes criticized as being too sensual. It inspiration, however, was never really been in doubt. The misdirected criticisms of sensuality do not understand the purpose of the book, which is to emphasize the nobility of marriage.

Ezekiel

There were some who considered the Book of Ezekiel to be against the Mosaic Law. However, no specific examples were ever provided. The problem was again one of interpretation, not inspiration.

Proverbs

Proverbs had some who doubted it because of certain supposed inner contradictions. Yet a proper interpretation of the book will show this is not the case.

WHY WAS THE AUTHORITY OF CERTAIN NEW TESTAMENT BOOKS QUESTIONED?

Some of the books that are now in the New Testament canon have been, at times, questioned as being inspired of God. They are known as the *antilegomena*, "the books spoken against." There were seven books whose authority was doubted by some members of the early church. The reasons vary from book to book.

Hebrews

The main problem that some of the early church members had with the Book of Hebrews was that it was written anonymously. Yet Hebrews is not the only anonymous New Testament book; the four Gospels, for instance, do not name their authors either. From the earliest times, the letter to the Hebrews was accepted everywhere but in Latin Christianity. The problem still was lack of a stated author. However, it was soon realized that the Book of Hebrews was orthodox in its content and deserved a place in the New Testament.

James

The main problem some had with James was the content. James put more emphasis on works than do the other New Testament writings. But James is not so much theological as it is practical and fits a much-needed gap between the doctrine and practice of Christianity.

Second Peter

The most suspect of all the books is 2 Peter. Basically, the reasons for questioning its authorship are the stylistic differences between it and 1 Peter. However, these stylistic differences can be explained by Peter's use of an *amanuensis*, or secretary, to do the writing for him.

Second and Third John

Second and Third John were questioned for several reasons. First, the author was not specifically stated he is called merely "the elder." Both letters were addressed to individuals, both are very brief, and neither have much theological content. Because of these factors there were not too many early writers who would quote from them.

Jude

Jude is a brief letter that gained immediate acceptance everywhere except Parthia, modern-day Iran. Jude was questioned for his use of the apocryphal Book of Enoch.

Revelation

It is no surprise that the Book of Revelation would meet some opposition due to the apocalyptic nature of the work. However, it had almost instant recognition everywhere except in Parthia. The great biblical scholar R. H. Charles wrote concerning the Book of Revelation:

> Throughout the Christian church during the second century, there is hardly any other book in the New Testament so well received as Revelation (R. H. Charles, Revelation, *The International Critical Commentary*, vol. 1, Edinburgh: T& T Clark, 1906).

We must remember that Jesus promised His disciples would be guided into all truth. The authority of Jesus' disciples matched that of Himself. Those whose writings were accepted by them would share the same authority. These seven books were only questioned by some of the church, not all of it. They were eventually recognized by the whole church to be included in the New Testament canon.

WHAT ARE THE APOCRYPHA?

There are a group of writings which are considered part of Old Testament Scripture by the Roman Catholic church but are not accepted as inspired by the Protestant church and Judaism. These are known as the Apocrypha.

The word Apocrypha means "hidden." The Apocrypha refers to the fifteen books (fourteen if the Letter of Jeremiah is put with Baruch) written between the years 300 B.C. and 100 B.C. (except Esdras which was written about A.D. 100). Eleven of these fourteen books are considered Holy Scripture by the Roman Catholic church. When added to the Old Testament, they constitute only seven extra books because the others are attached to existing books. The Apocrypha is about the size of the New Testament.

Apocrypha and Apocryphal

Sometimes people confuse the terms *Apocrypha* and *apocryphal*. The term *apocryphal* is also applied to other books that are New Testament forgeries. An example of this would be the Gospel of Thomas, which claims to have been written by Jesus' disciple Thomas. The book, however is a forgery. The word *Apocrypha* is a specific term used to refer to the particular books that are considered Scripture by the Roman Catholic Church.

History

The Protestant reformers, particularly in the sixteenth century, pointed out many abuses in the Roman Catholic church at that time. From 1545 to 1563 a church council met at Trent to answer some of their charges. Among their decisions was the pronouncement of these books as Holy Scripture. Before that time they were not regarded by the Roman Catholic church as sacred Scripture. The Protestant church rejects them for the following reasons:

No Claim

The primary reason for rejecting the Apocrypha as Scripture is that there is no claim within the books that they are inspired by God. This is in contrast to the canonical Scriptures which claim to record the revelation of God.

Never Cited

Though the New Testament cites directly or alludes to almost every book of the Old Testament as Scripture, it never cites the Apocrypha as being God's Word. If the Apocrypha were considered Scripture by the people living in the first century, we would certainly expect them to refer to it in some way.

The New Testament does refer to the Apocrypha in Jude 14 and Hebrews 11:35, but does not cite it as holy Scripture. It cites the works the same way Paul cited heathen poets (Acts 17:28). This demonstrates that the New Testament writers were familiar with the Apocrypha but did not consider them to be upon the same level as Old Testament Scripture.

Rejected by the Jews

The Jews have never considered these works to be inspired. On the contrary, they denied their inspiration. At the time of Christ we have the testimony of the Jewish writer Flavius Josephus that they were only twenty-two books to be inspired by God. The books of the Apocrypha were not among these.

Not on Early Lists

In the early years of the church it drew up various lists of the books it considered to be Scripture. The books of the Apocrypha do not appear on any list until the fourth century.

Rejected by Many Catholic Scholars

Many Roman Catholic scholars, through the Protestant Reformation, rejected the Apocrypha as Scripture. There was no unanimity of opinion among them that these books should be considered Scripture.

Demonstrable Errors

The Apocrypha also contains demonstrable errors. For example, Tobit was supposedly alive when Jereboam staged his revolt in 931 B.C. and was still alive when the Assyrians captured the Northern kingdom of Israel in 721 B.C. This means that he lived over two hundred years! However, the Book of Tobit says he lived only 158 years (Tobit 1:3-5; 14:11). This is an obvious contradiction. Other examples could be cited. Those who believe in an inerrant Scripture cannot accept the Apocrypha as God's Word.

No Evidence of Inspiration

The books of the Apocrypha do not contain anything like predictive prophecy that would give evidence of their inspiration. If these books were inspired by God, then we should expect to see some internal evidence confirming it. But there is none.

Old Testament Complete

It is clear that in the first century the Old Testament was complete. The Hebrews accepted the same thirty-nine books, (although divided differently) that the Protestant church does today. Jesus put His stamp of approval on these books but said nothing concerning the Apocrypha. However, He did say that the Scriptures were the authoritative Word of God and could not be broken. Any adding to that which God has revealed is denounced in the strongest of terms. Therefore, we have the testimony of Jesus against the authenticity of the Apocrypha.

We conclude that the Apocrypha should not be considered canonical because the books do not demonstrate themselves to be the upon the same level as Scripture. Jesus did not consider the part of His Old Testament and we are told not to add or subtract anything from God's Word.

DID JUDE QUOTE FROM THE BOOK OF ENOCH?

The Book of Jude seemingly contains a quotation of the intertestamental Book of Enoch. The question results from a citation found in Jude 14.

> Now Enoch, the seventh from Adam, prophesied about these men saying, 'Behold, the Lord comes with ten thousands of His saints' (Jude 14).

Jude records a prophecy made by Enoch, who lived before the flood of Noah. Enoch predicted the coming of the Lord to judge wicked individuals. The Apostle Paul wrote of this same judgment (2 Thessalonians 1:7-10). This prophecy made by Enoch is not recorded in the Old Testament. Two questions arise: (1) Where did Jude obtain his information? (2) Was Jude's information correct?

During the period between the testaments the Book of Enoch was written. It contains this prophecy. Some assume that Jude obtained this prophecy from the Book of Enoch, but this is not the case. Jude does not quote from the Book of Enoch but rather directly from Enoch. This could have been by means of special revelation from God or from some now unknown written source. The source of Jude's quotation was the person Enoch. Where the Book of Enoch derived his information is another matter. It is possible that the source of the quotation found in the Book of Enoch was Jude, since there is no evidence as to the precise contents of the Book of Enoch until several centuries *after* Jude was written. Whatever the answer may be, it is not necessary to assume that Jude considered the Book of Enoch as authoritative.

Since we believe that Jude's writing was inspired by God, we take this information as being correct. It is not essential to know how Jude obtained this information. Jesus had promised that His disciples would be indwelt by the Holy Spirit, who would guide them into all truth.

> However, when He, the Spirit of truth, has come, He will guide you into all truth; for He will not speak on His own authority, but whatever He hears He will speak (John 16:13).

Because of Jesus' promise, the words of the New Testament writers were safeguarded from error.

We conclude that Jude did not quote from the Book of Enoch, but received the information in some other way.

WHAT ABOUT OTHER BOOKS THAT CLAIM BIBLICAL AUTHORITY?

Throughout the history of the church many documents surfaced that claimed to have been written by the apostles or those intimately familiar with the life of Christ. However these works were written by someone other than the named author. These fraudulent works are known as the *pseudepigrapha* (forgeries). They are also known as apocryphal works, and were rejected by all. The early church father, Eusebius, called these books "totally absurd and impious." Over three hundred different works that fit into this category have been catalogued.

Other Gospels

Among the forgeries were a large number of apocryphal or false gospels. Origen, a third century writer, testified to the existence of other gospels when he wrote, "There are many who have tried to write gospels, but not all have been accepted."

The biblical scholar Edwin Yamauchi offers an appropriate comment:

> The apocryphal gospels are non-canonical writings of a motely variety about the purported deeds and revelations of Jesus Christ. Though the Greek word apocrypha originally meant "hidden," the church fathers used it to describe spurious writings foisted as gospels.

> Irenaeus refers to 'an unspeakable number of apocryphal and spurious writings, which they themselves (i. e. the heretics) had forged to bewilder the minds of the foolish.' Although some of them were patterned after the canonical gospels, many bear little resemblance to them. As Origen noted, 'The Church possesses four Gospels, heresy a great many' (Edwin M. Yamauchi, "The Word From Nag Hammadi," *Christianity Today*, January 13, 1978, p. 19).

Gnostic Influence

Many of these works were influenced by gnosticism. The word gnostic means "one who has knowledge." The gnostics taught that salvation came by secret knowledge of God. The gnostic view of God is contrary to the Bible. In addition, the gnostics considered that all matter is evil.

An example of gnostic writing can be found in the Gospel of Philip. The original Gospel of Philip was probably written sometime during the second century A.D. The influence of gnosticism and its emphasis on secret knowledge can be clearly seen in this work. The Gospel of Philip reads,

> The Logos said: If you know the truth the truth will make you free. Ignorance is a slave, knowledge is freedom. When we recognize the truth we shall find the fruits of truth in our hearts. If we unite with it, we will bring our fulfillment.

Different Level

Other statements show that they are on a different level than Scripture.

> A Gentile man does not die, for he has never lived that he should die. Adam came into being from two virgins, from the Spirit and from the virgin earth. Because of this Christ was born of a virgin, in order that he might set in order the stumbling which came to pass at the beginning.

These fanciful statements betray their non-biblical source.

Second-Hand Sources

The pseudepigrapha, apart from being forgeries, were also written long after, in some cases hundreds of years after, the New Testament events. The writers were not eyewitnesses to the life of Christ or to the events of the early church. This is another reason to reject the testimony which they give.

Gospel of Thomas

One of the most prominent of all the forgeries in the Gospel of Thomas. The Gospel of Thomas was probably composed in Edessa in Syria about A.D. 140. Consisting of 114 sayings of Jesus, it is the most extensive collection of non-biblical sayings of Jesus that still exist. The Gospel of Thomas begins as follows:

> These are the secret words which the living Jesus spoke and Didymus Judas Thomas wrote. And He said: Whosoever finds the explanation of these words shall not taste death.

We know that the Gospel of Thomas is a forgery for the following reasons:

Incorrect Name

The author is not Thomas. Whoever wrote the Gospel of Thomas used the incorrect name when referring to the Apostle Thomas as Didymus Judas Thomas. In the four Gospels, Thomas is referred to as either Didymus or Thomas, not both at once. Didymus is the word for "twin" in both Greek and Aramaic, so the author of the Gospel of Thomas must not have been aware of this linguistic collection.

Secret Approach

The secret approach found in the Gospel of Thomas is typical of the writings of the gnostics. The four Gospels are open about the ways of salvation and the kingdom of God while the Gospel of Thomas views truth from a hidden vantage point.

There is no historical setting for the statements. The Gospel of Thomas is a compilation of sayings without the inclusion of important historical events as recorded in the Gospels. We are not told when or under what circumstances the statements were made.

Contradicts Four Gospels

Many of the sayings are contradictory to those we have in the Gospels. For example, saying 114 says:

> Jesus said, 'See, I shall lead her, so that I will make her male, that she too many become a living spirit, resembling you males. For every woman who makes herself male will enter the Kingdom of Heaven.'

Different Jesus

The person of Jesus Christ is different than the one revealed in the Gospels. In the Gospels Jesus is God the Son, Second Person of the Trinity. In the Gospel of Thomas He is one who points the way by which an individual can attain the knowledge of God.

These reasons demonstrate that the Gospel of Thomas is a forgery rather than a legitimate work written by one of Jesus' apostles.

Aquarian Gospel of Jesus Christ

One alternative explanation of the life and ministry of Jesus that has caused considerable interest is the Aquarian Gospel of Jesus the Christ. This work was written by Levi Dowling (1844-1911), based upon communication he received from an alleged "universal mind." The Aquarian Gospel attempts to fill in some of the missing years of Jesus' youth as well as explain His wisdom by attributing it to contact with holy men of other religions. The result is a contradictory mixture of Christian science and occultic thought.

The name is derived from the astrological idea that a new Aquarian age has come upon us, bringing with it the need for a new spiritual gospel, the Aquarian gospel.

Content

The Aquarian Gospel of Jesus the Christ attempts to fill in some of the blanks in the life of Jesus. Some of the material in the Aquarian Gospel is borrowed from the ancient Gospel of James, a well-known forgery in the early years of the church. The most prominent part of the book deals with the education and travel of Jesus. According to the Aquarian Gospel, Jesus first studied under the Jewish teacher Hillel and then went to India to spend time with their holy men. His learning also supposedly took Him to Tibet, Persia, Assyria, Greece, and Egypt. It was in Egypt that Jesus was said to have joined the sacred brotherhood. He passed through seven degrees and emerged as the Logos. In Alexandria a council of seven sages was held where they formulated seven great religious postulates and ordained Jesus for the work of the ministry.

The Aquarian Gospel then rewrites the four gospels according to its own particular viewpoint. The end of the story has Jesus appearing in a materialized body to people in India, Persia, Greece, and other countries.

Evaluation

Like many previous attempts, the Aquarian Gospel attempts to give an explanation of the wisdom and character of Jesus apart from the biblical depiction. Dowling's reconstruction shows obvious borrowing from the Ancient Gospel of James, as well as familiarity with a nineteenth century works, Novotitch's "Unknown Life of Jesus Christ."

The book begins with an historical inaccuracy: "Augustus Caesar reigned and Herod Antipas was ruler in Jerusalem." This is an error because Antipas ruled in Galilee, never in Jerusalem.

A crucial problem with the Aquarian Gospel concerns its scenario of the source of Jesus' teachings. If Jesus obtained His wisdom from the masters of India, Greece, and other countries, then why doesn't His teaching reflect it? The teachings of Jesus, as recorded in the Gospels, are in direct conflict with every central belief of Hinduism, Buddhism, and the other religions with which He supposedly came into contact!

The simple fact is that we have in the Gospels a first-hand account of the life and ministry of Jesus. The Aquarian Gospel is a false portrait of the life of Christ, not based upon historical records or eyewitness testimony but rather upon the recollections of an ancient forgery and the imagination of a twentieth-century writer. It has no value whatsoever in providing new or accurate information on the life of Christ.

The Archko Volume

One of the most famous written hoaxes is the Archko Volume. The work is also known as the "Report of Pilate" or "Archko Library." The content of this work is an alleged report of the trial and death of Jesus made by Pontius Pilate to the Emperor Tiberius. Its existence can be traced back to Rev. W. D. Mahan of Boonville, Missouri, who published a thirty-two page pamphlet in 1879 titled, "A Correct Transcript of Pilate's Court."

The success of the "Report of Pilate" led Mahan to make some more "discoveries" including: an interview with the shepherds who were given the announcement of Christ's birth, Gamaliel's interview with Joseph and Mary, Eli's story of the Magi, and other previously unknown interviews surrounding the life and ministry of Jesus. Mahan claimed these "interviews" were translated from ancient manuscripts in Rome or Constantinople.

Edgar Goodspeed writes concerning the accuracy of the "interviews":

> The picture of Jesus in his interview with Pilate is romantic and theatrical, and the Pilate reflected in the "Report" is historically improbable.
>
> The whole work is a weak, crude fancy, a jumble of high-sounding but meaningless words, and hardly worth serious criticism. It is difficult to see how it could have deceived anyone. . . . Like the "Report of Pilate," these [the other interviews] bristle with childish blunders. . . . The supposed references to Josephus's *Jewish Wars* . . . simply do not exist. The statement that Josephus in his *Antiquities* refers to Jesus in more than fifty places is false . . . That Tacitus wrote his history of Agricola in A.D. 56 is of course an error; Tacitus was born in 55, and even if he had been able to write his father-in-law's biography at the age of one year, there was nothing yet to write, for Agricola, for Agricola himself was only nineteen (Edgar Goodspeed, *Famous Biblical Hoaxes*, pp. 33, 35).

As can be imagined, the "Report of Pilate" as well as the later interviews were immediately exposed as frauds. It was noticed, for instance, that entire pages of Eli's story of the Magi were copied verbatim from the novel Ben Hur!

Unhappily, people continue to read and believe these fraudulent works although they have no basis in fact.

The Lost Books of the Bible

One of the most often asked questions concerns the so-called "Lost Books of the Bible." A book with this title was produced in 1926. It was the reprint of William Hone's *Apocryphal New Testament*, first printed in 1820. Hone's book was copied from two earlier one's published in 1736 and 1737. Thus the materials found in the "Lost Books of the Bible" were written 250 years ago. Since the time of the original writing of the lost books, the field of manuscript studies has made tremendous advances but none of this has been taken into account by those who publish these works.

The contents of the "lost books" include the following:

Four Infancy Gospels:

They include: "The Birth of Mary," a work written in the middle of the second century; "The Protoevangelium of James," written about the same time; the first "Gospel of Infancy," composed about A.D. 400; "The Second Infancy Gospel," which in reality is a fragment of the Gospel of Thomas.

These were so-called infancy gospels that were written to fill in the details of the early unrecorded years of the life of Christ. These works include stories of Jesus forming clay figures of animals and birds which He makes walk, fly, and eat. Another account has a child who runs into Jesus falling down dead. These examples are representative of the fanciful nature of the accounts.

The Letter of King Abgar

This was supposedly a letter written to Jesus by Abgar, King of Edessa. Jesus' reply to the letter is also contained. These works were written in the third century.

Gospel of Nicodemus

This is also known as "The Acts of Pilate." It was written in the fourth or fifth century.

Other works found among the lost books include the Apostles' Creed and the spurious letter from Paul to the Laodiceans.

These books have been called "outlaw" Scriptures by some. But this is not the case, for none of these works were ever thought of as part of the New Testament. Anyone who claims these works were suppressed by the church is speaking out of ignorance or a desire to deceive.

It is obvious from the date of composition of these works that they cannot be considered on the same plane as Holy Scripture, which was written by eyewitnesses or people who recorded eyewitness testimony of the life and ministry of Jesus.

Contrast With Four Gospels

One hundred years ago F.W. Farrar wrote the following that is still true today:

> The Four Gospels superseded all others and won their way into universal acceptance by their intrinsic value and authority. After so many salutary losses we still possess a rich collection of Apocryphal Gospels, and, if they serve no other good purpose, they have this value, that they prove for us undoubtedly the unique and transcendent superiority of the sacred records. These bear the stamp of absolute truthfulness, all the more decisively when placed in contrast with the writings which show signs of willful falsity. We escape their lying magic to find support and help from the genuine gospels. And here we take refuge with the greater confidence because the ruins which lie around the ancient archives of the Church look like a guarantee of the enduring strength and greatness of those archives themselves (F. W. Farrar, *The Messages of the Books*, p. 27).

A. Roberts and J. Donaldson, the editors of the Ante-Nicene Library, said the other gospels offer . . .

> curious glimpses of the state of the Christian conscience, and of modes of thought in the first centuries of our era; the predominant impression which they leave on our minds is the immeasurable superiority, the unapproachable simplicity and the majesty of the Canonical writings.

We conclude that any other book apart from the New Testament that attempts to fill in the gaps of the life of Christ only reveals the superiority of the four Gospels.

HAS GOD REVEALED ANYTHING FURTHER TO MANKIND SINCE THE FIRST CENTURY?

There is evidence that the canon of Scripture was complete in the first century. Has God, since that time, revealed anything that is to be added to Holy Scripture?

Claims Do Not Make It True

The mere claim that God spoke to an individual does not make it true. There has to be evidence to back up the claim. The question is, "Does the evidence support the claim that God spoke through them?" The Bible instructs us to test the spirits:

> Beloved, do not believe every spirit, but test the spirits whether they are of God; because many false prophets have gone out into the world (1 John 4:1).

When we test the claims of those who have brought forth a "new Scripture" we find them to be untrue.

The downfall of all the books that have had inspiration claimed for them is that they present a different revelation from what has previously been recorded. They contradict the Bible. For example, the Koran says that Jesus was not the Son of God and that He did not die upon the cross for the sins of the world.

The sacred books of Mormonism teach that there exist many gods rather than the one God the Bible speaks of. In addition, Mormonism teaches that each male can someday become a god himself. Mormonism also denies the doctrine of the Trinity, salvation by grace through faith, and the eternal punishment of the wicked.

No Book Qualifies

Every book written since the completion of the Bible that claims to be further revelation from God fails on the same ground. They all deny that Jesus Christ is God Himself, second Person of the Trinity. These works also deny salvation by grace through faith. They preached a different gospel. The Apostle Paul warned the church at Galatia about such people.

> I marvel that you are turning away so soon from Him who called you in the grace of Christ, to a different gospel . . . But even if we, or an angel from heaven, preach any other gospel to you than what we have preached to you, let him be accursed (Galatians 1:6,8).

No Evidence

Furthermore, there is no substantiating evidence such as fulfilled prophecy to demonstrate the books are of divine inspiration.

Thus, as we examine the various books that have been written since the completion of the New Testament that have claimed to be further revelation from God, we find them coming short of the mark. The Bible warns:

> Every word of God is pure; He is a shield to those who put their trust in Him. Do not add to His words, lest He reprove you and you be found a liar (Proverbs 30:5,6).

CAN ANYTHING BE ADDED TO THE BIBLE TODAY?

We have seen that the canon was closed in the first century, and that since then God has not revealed anything on the level with Holy Scripture.

Westminster Confession

The Westminster Confession, a seventeenth-century statement of faith, says concerning the Bible,

> The whole counsel of God, concerning all things necessary for His own glory, man's salvation, faith and life, is either expressly set down in Scripture, or by good and necessary consequence may be deduced from Scripture: unto which nothing at any time is to be added, whether by new revelations of the Spirit, or traditions of men (Westminster Confession 1:10).

According to this statement, which sums up the Protestant view of Scripture, nothing is to be added or subtracted from the Bible. The revelation from God to man has been completed.

No Direct Word

However, there is no direct word in the Bible that says God has stopped revealing Himself. Some have appealed to the following verses in the Book of Revelation.

> For I testify to everyone who hears the words of the prophecy of this book: If anyone adds to these things, God will add to him the plagues that are written in this book; and if anyone takes away from the words of the book of this prophecy, God shall take away his part from the Book of Life (Revelation 22:18,19).

This is only speaking of the Book of Revelation. It is not a commandment against adding any other book to Scripture. If taken literally, then you could not have any other book in Scripture but the Book of Revelation!

Yet there is a principle here that is clearly taught. No one is to add or to take away from the revealed Word of God.

Jude makes a statement that is pertinent to our discussion.

> I found it necessary to write to you exhorting you to contend earnestly for the faith which has one for all delivered to the saints (Jude 3).

This verse teaches that a body of truth from God has been delivered to man and that this faith has been wholly delivered. This seems to indicate that no further revelation from God is necessary. God has told us in Scripture everything that we need to know about who He is, who we are, and what will happen to the earth in the future.

We know the nature of God does not change:

> For I am the Lord, I do not change (Malachi 3:6).

The Bible says clearly that the faith has been completely revealed. Therefore, if any new revelation were to come from God, it would be consistent with past revelations.

Even if a work met all of the above criteria, it would not necessarily be the Word of God. While theoretically it is possible that God could add something to what He has previously revealed, it is highly unlikely that this would be the case. The faith has already been delivered to mankind. Any further word from God to man is not necessary. The canon of Scripture is complete.

CONCLUSION ON PART 5

After considering the subject of the canon of Scripture we can make the following conclusions.

1. The term canon refers to the authoritative books of Scripture.

2. God is the One who decided which books should be placed in the Bible.

3. We know the correct books are in the Bible because of the testimony of Jesus.

4. The Apocrypha, books considered inspired by the Roman Catholic church, do not give evidence of inspiration.

5. Recent books that have claimed Divine inspiration have proven themselves to be frauds.

6. The Scripture is complete. Nothing should be added or subtracted from it.

We now come to our last section which deals with the interpretation and application of the Scripture. In Part 6 we will examine the differences between a translation and a paraphrase, look at why there are so many Bible translations, and consider some principles for correctly interpreting the Word of God.

PART 6

INTERPRETATION AND APPLICATION

WHAT IS A TRANSLATION (VERSION)?

The word translation can be defined as the process of transferring the meaning of a word, phrase, or idea from one language to another. A Bible translation is the rendering of the text of the Bible into a language other than that which it was originally written.

We need to remember that the Bible was originally written in three different languages. The Old Testament was mainly written in Hebrew with a small portion composed in Aramaic. The New Testament was originally written in Greek. Whenever the Bible is expressed in a language other than these, it is a translation.

Translations are made in order to help the reader better understand the Word of God. Not everyone has the time, or capacity, to learn the original languages in which the Scriptures were written.

The translation of the Scripture has been going on for a long time. When the Jews returned from the Babylonian captivity, they used the Scripture to help reunite the nation. The scribe Ezra read the Scripture to the people and then explained it to them (Nehemiah 8). This was necessary because these people no longer understood the form of Hebrew in which the Old Testament books were written. They were speaking Aramaic.

Sometime later, about 250 B.C., the Hebrew Scriptures were translated into Greek. This version is known as the Septuagint. The reason for this translation was the desire to make the Hebrew Scriptures understandable to Greek-speaking people.

Soon after the New Testament was written, it was translated into Latin, Syriac, and other languages. This practice has continued until the present. For example, the Bible has been translated from the original languages into English for the benefit of people in English-speaking nations who wish to know and study God's Word. Present-day translations into modern English help people accomplish the task of understanding God's Word.

WHAT IS A PARAPHRASE?

We have seen that a translation attempts to render Scripture into another language. A paraphrase, on the other hand, is not a literal rendering of the original text, but is more of a commentary. The purpose of a paraphrase is to put the ideas of one language into another without writing down the word-by-word meaning of the original.

The following example will readily show the difference between a translation and a paraphrase. We will see how two translations render 1 Kings 20:11 and then observe how a paraphrase deals with the same verse. The King James reads:

> Let not him that girdeth on his harness boast himself as he that putteth it off.

This is a literal translation, but the meaning is certainly not clear to twentieth-century readers.

The New American Standard Bible also translated this verse literally,

> Let not him who girds on his armor boast like him who takes it off.

This is a bit more understandable than the King James Version.

The Living Bible, a paraphrase, reads,

> Don't count your chickens before they hatch.

One can readily see that the paraphrase makes the passage easier to understand, even though the rendering has no word-for-word association with the original.

Use of Paraphrases

A paraphrase has a definite purpose in the understanding of the Bible. However, it should not be used in place of a translation. A paraphrase should rather be used in conjunction with a translation. When used alongside a translation, it can amplify the meaning of the text to the reader. It then becomes a tool for the further understanding of Scripture. A paraphrase can be helpful in that it introduces new readers to Bible study with less labor on their part. In addition, a paraphrase is good for less skilled and younger readers.

WHY HAVE THERE BEEN SO MANY TRANSLATIONS?

New translations of the Bible are necessary for the following reasons.

Change in Language

One of the reasons for new translations is change of language. Languages are not static, they are always in a state of flux. New translations must be written in order to let the people read the Word of God in their contemporary language.

With the passage of time, some words change in meaning. There are many English words that have a different meaning today from their meaning in the King James Version of 1611. For example, the King James Version has Jesus saying, "Suffer the little children to come unto me" (Mark 10:14). In the seventeenth century the word *suffer* had the meaning of "allow" or "permit." Yet many modern-day readers would not be aware of this fact because the word suffer now has an altogether different meaning. Many other words have changed meaning as well. So it is important to update translations to fit the current usage of the language.

New Manuscript Discoveries

In times past, new manuscript discoveries called for a fresh translation of the Scriptures. When the King James

Version was translated in 1611, only a few Greek manuscripts were available to use in translating the New Testament. Today over 5,500 Greek manuscripts have been catalogued. Though the translation remains virtually the same, there are minor changes in some details.

Same Account

It cannot be too greatly emphasized that every translation, except for a corrupt few, says virtually the same thing. This is because the text behind the translation has not appreciably changed. All one must do is compare the renderings of different verses or passages in different translations and one will be readily see that the message is always the same. The great number of Bible translations should not cause anyone to lose confidence in God's Word.

WHAT MAKES A GOOD TRANSLATION?

We have mentioned that there are many good translations of the Bible. The ultimate test of a good translation is faithfulness to the original text. But what if a person does not know Greek or Hebrew? How can one know whether a translation has been faithful to the original? The following guidelines should be applied:

Comparison

The reader should compare translations. As he does this, he will immediately notice that most of them will be very much alike. Those that differ radically from the majority should not be considered reliable.

Bible Helps

There are many Bible helps that can aid the reader in deciding upon the best translation. Lexicons, Bible encyclopedias, and concordances all provide help in understanding the meaning of a passage.

The preface of almost every translation of Scripture lists guidelines by which the translators set about their work. The reader should find out what these guidelines were. Questions that should be answered are: "Why was the translation made? What specific things were they trying to accomplish?"

Readability

Another thing the reader should look for is a translation that he understands. Does the translation convey the message to him in an understandable way? Each reader will have his own particular likes or dislikes concerning different translations. Some will prefer the more literary translations while others will desire more straightforward, literal renderings. While this should not be the only criterion used in choosing a Bible, it should be a consideration.

Test of Time

Many new translations of the Bible attempt to reach particular groups of people by "using their own language." Unfortunately, due to the changes in language, most of these translations are out of date by the time they are printed. This type of translation is not recommended. A good translation will stand the test of time.

What modern day translations would meet the above qualifications? The author recommends the New American Standard Bible and the New King James Version. These are good translations of Scripture, excellent for personal study.

HOW IS A PERSON SUPPOSED TO INTERPRET THE BIBLE?

A person should keep in mind several principles of interpretation when studying the Bible.

The primary rule in interpreting any communication is to try and find what the author intended. Thus, when it comes to Scripture, our primary goal should be to attempt to understand what the author, God, is trying to communicate.

Literal Meaning

We have established the fact that the Bible is God's communication to mankind. Obviously, if the Bible intends to reach the maximum number of people, then the message should be understood at face value. The Bible should be interpreted in a literal manner. Charles Horne expounds on this idea:

> In common life, no prudent and conscientious person, who either commits his sentiments to writing or utters anything, intends that a diversity of meanings should be attached to what he writes or says; and consequently, neither his readers, nor those who hear him, affix to it any other than the true and obvious sense. . . The literal sense of any place of Scripture is that which the words signify, or require, in their natural and proper acceptation, without any . . . metaphor, or figure, and abstracted from mystic meaning (Charles Horne, *An Introduction To The Critical Study and Knowledge of*

> *Scriptures*, cited by Bernard Ramm, *Protestant Biblical Interpretation*, Grand Rapids, Baker Book House, 1970}, p. 107).

Interpreted as Other Books

Another point that needs to be made is that the Bible should be interpreted by the same rules we use to interpret any other book. There are no special rules we should consider when we interpret the Bible. The Old Testament authority, Walter Kaiser, has written:

> Man's basic ability to interpret is not derived from some science, technical skill, or exotic course open only to the more gifted intellects of a society. The general principles of interpreting are not learned, invented, or discovered by people. They are part and parcel of the nature of man as a being made in the image of God. Given the gift of communication and speech itself, man has already begun to practice the principles of hermeneutics [the science of interpretation]. The art has been in use from the moment God spoke to Adam in the Garden, and from the time Adam addressed Eve, until the present. In human conversation the speaker is always the author; the person spoken to is always the interpreter. Correct understanding must always begin with the meaning the speaker attaches to his own words (cited by Norman Geisler, ed., *Inerrancy*, Grand Rapids, Zondervan, 1980, p. 120).

The Bible should be approached like all other books with regard to interpretation. We should seek to identify the author's intent and take the words in their literal meaning.

Interpret Contextually

The Bible should also be interpreted contextually. This means the context should be studied in order to see how each verse relates to that which precedes and that which follows. Close attention should be paid to the theme and scope of the biblical book under consideration.

Compare Scripture with Scripture

It is also important to compare Scripture with Scripture. As already mentioned, each writer did not necessarily understand the full import of what he was recording. We must remember that the ultimate author behind each of the books of the Bible is God. When Scripture is compared with Scripture we can then discover the full implications of what God intended.

Progressive Revelation

In addition, the interpreter needs to recognize the progressive character of God's revelation. God may add or change certain things He previously revealed. For example, the Old Testament forbids the people to eat pork. This commandment is rescinded in the New Testament (see Acts 10; 1 Timothy 4:3). Failure to recognize that God has revealed His Word progressively will cause all sorts of problems with interpretation.

These points should be kept in mind when interpreting God's Word.

WHAT HELPS DO TRANSLATIONS PROVIDE FOR STUDYING THE BIBLE?

Modern translations have provided many helpful features that allow the reader to better study the Scripture. They include chapter and verse divisions, italics, and marginal notes.

Chapter and Verse Divisions

The chapter and verse divisions were not in the original manuscripts. They were added later to make easier the finding and reading of passages. The Bible was divided into chapters in 1227 by Stephen Langton, a professor at the University of Paris and later Archbishop of Canterbury. Verse division was done by the French printer Robert Stephanus (Stephens) for his Greek New Testament published in 1551. The first entire Bible in which these chapter and verse divisions were used was Stephen's edition of the Latin Vulgate (1555). The first English New Testament to have both chapter and verse divisions was the Geneva Bible (1560).

The chapter and verse divisions are convenient for reference and quotation purposes. Yet it must be remembered that they are man-made, sometimes arbitrary, and they sometimes interfere with the sense of the passage. They should be disregarded in various kinds of Bible study. The first step in interpretation is to ignore the modern chapter and verse division.

Italics

The use of italics first appeared in the Geneva Bible (1557-1560) and have been used in translations ever since. The words in italic letters are not used for emphasis but to indicate words not found in the original. These words are supplied by the translators in an effort to make clear the meaning of the passage. In many cases they are necessary. Sometimes, however, they can give a wrong sense of the original. Ordinarily they can be tested by reading the passage through without the italics and then reading the passage with the italics. If the italics give the passage another meaning, or weaken what is stated, it is safe to omit them. If they do not change the meaning but simply clarify it then the italics should be retained.

Marginal Notes

The marginal notes written in our Bibles are valuable for several reasons.

(1) They explain the meaning of proper names and other Greek and Hebrew words retained in the text. (2) Marginal notes also explain words relating to money, weights and measures. (3) They can also help alternative renderings of Hebrew and Greek words.

(4) Marginal notes can also suggest a more literal or exact meaning of the word or phrase. (5) Marginal notes also are helpful in explaining some obscure idiom or custom. (6) Marginal notes also give different renderings found in other versions of the Bible.

These three features, contained in most modern translations, serve as interpretive aids in better understanding the message of Scripture.

DO WE NEED SOMEONE TO INTERPRET THE BIBLE FOR US?

Is it necessary for some sort of spiritual authority figure to interpret the Bible for ordinary people? The answer is no. God has spoken to us in such a clear way in the Bible that we do not need someone to tell us what it means.

Everyone should read and study the Bible. The Apostle Paul wrote to Timothy,

> Be diligent to present yourself approved to God, a worker who does not need to be ashamed, rightly dividing the word of truth (2 Timothy 2:15).

Gift of Teaching

Though the basic message of Scripture is clear for all people, God has gifted some to teach to His people. Paul lists teaching among the spiritual gifts of the church:

> And God has appointed these in the church: first apostles, second prophets, third teachers (1 Corinthians 12:28).

God has provided teachers for the purpose of instructing believers and leading them into maturity in the faith. People are instructed to listen to teachers.

> Obey, those who rule over you, and be submissive, for they watch out for your souls, as those who must give

> account. Let them do so with joy and not with grief, for they would be unprofitable for you (Hebrews 13:17).

However, they are not to exercise absolute authority over believers. Simon Peter wrote:

> Shepherd the flock of God which is among you, serving as overseers, not by constraint but willingly, not for dishonest gain but eagerly; not as being lords over those entrusted to you, but being examples to the flock (1 Peter 5:2,3).

Hence, those who teach are to be examples to their listeners. They are not to lord over the people as tyrants but rather are to help bring their hearers to maturity "in Christ."

Teachers, we conclude, are necessary for the growth and development of believers, but they are not essential for people to understand the basic message of Scripture.

ARE ACCOUNTS LIKE ADAM AND EVE, NOAH, DANIEL AND JONAH TO BE UNDERSTOOD LITERALLY?

Are we to understand all the events that Scripture records as literally occurring? Do we have to believe in a literal Adam and Eve? Noah's flood? Jonah? Daniel?

The answer is yes. These four accounts, which have caused so much controversy regarding their historicity, were all confirmed by Jesus as having literally occurred.

Adam and Eve

Jesus used Adam and Eve as an illustration of marriage and divorce.

> Have you not read that He who made them at the beginning made them male and female? (Matthew 19:4).

He assumed they literally existed.

Noah

The flood of Noah was used by Jesus as a sign of His Second Coming.

> As it was in the days of Noah, so it will be also in the days of the Son of Man (Luke 17:26).

Daniel

Modern liberal scholars do not accept Daniel as the author of the book bearing his name because the Book of Daniel contains prophecies that were fulfilled in their minutest details. However, Jesus verified the fact that Daniel was a prophet, referring to "the 'abomination of desolation,' spoken of by Daniel the prophet" (Matthew 24:15).

Jonah

The story of Jonah is often held up to ridicule, yet Jesus used the account of Jonah and the great fish as a sign of His resurrection.

> For as Jonah was three days and three nights in the belly of the great fish, so will the Son of Man be three days and three nights in the heart of the earth. The men of Nineveh will rise in the judgment with this generation and condemn it, because they repented at the preaching of Jonah (Matthew 12:40,41).

We conclude that the Bible treats these accounts as having literally occurred. It is as if Jesus realized that these four accounts would receive much attention from unbelieving critics of the Bible, and so He made a point to verify their accuracy.

WHAT IS ILLUMINATION?

One important teaching ministry of the Holy Spirit is illumination. Illumination can be defined as that which occurs when a truth of Scripture is made understandable by the Holy Spirit to the individual. Therefore, illumination has to do with the proper interpretation of Scripture.

Inspiration and Illumination

There is an important difference between inspiration and illumination. Inspiration is the Holy Spirit's active influence on the authors of Scripture that led them to put God's Word into writing. Illumination is the gift given to every believer to be able to interpret God's revelation. Unbelievers cannot experience the illumination of the Holy Spirit. Though they may intellectually understand what the Bible says, they considers the message as foolish.

Promise

The Bible says that the Holy Spirit will lead the believer into all truth:

> However, when He, the Spirit of truth, has come, He will guide you into all truth, for He will not speak on His own authority, but whatever He hears He will speak; and He will tell you things to come (John 16:13).

The Spirit's teaching consists of "all truth" including "things to come," prophecy.

The Witness of the Spirit

The ability to understand the Scripture is a gift from the Holy Spirit.

> For what man knows the things of a man except the spirit of the man which is in him? Even so no one knows the things of God except the Spirit of God (1 Corinthians 2:11).

For Believers Only

God has given the Holy Spirit to all those who believe in Jesus Christ:

> And because you are sons, God has sent forth the Spirit of His Son into your hearts (Galatians 4:6).

As a person grows in his Christian faith, his ability to understand the Bible increases. Scripture encourages the believer to grow in Christ.

> As newborn babes, desire the pure milk of the word, that you may grow thereby (1 Peter 2:2).

Therefore, it is through the illuminating ministry of the Holy Spirit that a believer grows in his faith and is able to properly interpret the Word of God. The ultimate purpose of the teaching ministry of the Holy Spirit is to glorify Jesus Christ.

WHAT IS TYPOLOGY?

One of the ways the New Testament is understood is through typology, the study of types. A type can be defined as a shadow cast on the pages of Old Testament history by a truth that is fully revealed in the New Testament. Many Old Testament events have a far-reaching significance, for they speak of something to be fulfilled in the future. The Apostle Paul, in referring to Old Testament events, wrote:

> Now all these things happened to them as examples, and they were written for our admonition, on whom the end of the ages have come (1 Corinthians 10:11).

The following characteristics can be found in types:

Historical

The biblical types have their basis in history. Although they speak of a future event, the type itself was an actual historical occurrence. For example, Jonah's experience with the great fish as a type of the death and resurrection of Christ. Jesus said:

> And no sign will be given to it (this generation) except the sign of the prophet Jonah. For as Jonah was three days and three nights in the belly of the great fish, so will the Son of Man be three days and three nights in the heart of the earth (Matthew 12:39,40).

Jonah's experience, though it typified the resurrection of Christ, was a historical event.

Prophetic

Types are always prophetic. They speak of events that are still to come. Melchizedek was a historical figure (Genesis 14) whose life spoke of Christ. The Book of Hebrews testifies that Melchizedek, "without father, without mother, without genealogy, having neither beginning of days nor end of life, but made like the Son of God, remains a priest continually" (Hebrews 7:3).

They Speak of Christ

Types all point, in one way to another, to the person of Jesus Christ. The Apostle Paul writing to the church at Corinth, spoke of the experiences of the children of Israel in the wilderness:

> And all drank the same spiritual drink. For they drank of that spiritual Rock that followed them, and that Rock was Christ (1 Corinthians 10:4).

Paul says the rock from which the people drank represented Jesus Christ. He then went on to say,

> Now these things became our examples, to the intent that we should not lust after evil things as they also lusted (1 Corinthians 10:6).

We must, however, be careful of extremes. Some people have carried the study of typology further than the Bible legitimately allows. We must be restrained in our quest to find types in the Old Testament history.

WHY DO SO MANY PEOPLE INTERPRET THE BIBLE DIFFERENTLY?

One of the main arguments people use to avoid accepting the Bible as an authoritative source is that so many interpret it differently. Does this mean there is no consensus of opinion as to what the Bible says? Not at all. There is a consensus of opinion as to what the Bible means. Three points need to be made clear.

Common Belief

The three main branches of Christendom—Protestantism, Eastern Orthodox, and Roman Catholicism—all accept the Apostles' Creed. They all agree upon the fact that Jesus Christ was God in human flesh, born of the virgin Mary, that He lived a sinless life upon the earth, and that He demonstrated His authority by performing many signs and wonders. They also teach that Jesus was crucified under Pontius Pilate for the sins of the world, and then rose again upon the third day. Furthermore, they believe and teach that someday Jesus will come back to judge the living and the dead. On these issues there is no disagreement.

Secondary Issues

The differences that groups hold are on secondary issues, not primary ones. The major branches of

Christianity, as well as the denominations, are not separated by issues that are vital to the faith. Christianity is united upon much more than it is divided over.

The Message is Clear

The third and last point is that the message of the Bible is clear. Martin Luther wrote,

> I certainly grant that many passages in the Scriptures are obscure and hard to elucidate, but that is due, not to the exalted nature of the subject, but to our own linguistic and grammatical ignorance; and it does not in any way prevent us knowing all the contents of Scripture.

It cannot be too strongly stressed that the unbelievers of Jesus' time did not reject His message because they did not understand it. They knew exactly what He said, but they refused to believe it. The problem was not lack of understanding, but lack of faith. The same holds true today.

The common excuse—that there are so many ways to interpret the Bible that no one can be sure what it means—is not valid. The message of the Bible is clear, and God is going to hold each person responsible based upon how he reacts to that message.

HOW CAN A PERSON KNOW THE BIBLE IS THE WORD OF GOD?

In this book we have answered questions about the reliability and historical accuracy of the Bible. We saw that the text has been accurately transmitted throughout history. The texts of the Old and New Testaments read the same today as when they were originally written. The evidence also led us to conclude that the history recorded in the pages of Scripture is accurate. However, this still does not make the Bible the Word of God.

This brings up the final question: How can a person know if God has spoken? We offer the following evidence for anyone considering the Bible's claim to be the God's Word.

Establish Reliability

The first thing that needs to be done is to establish the reliability of the biblical text. This can be done by applying the same procedures used in investigating any historical text. When the evidence is evaluated, the Bible shows itself to be a trustworthy document. The text of the Bible has been handed down without suffering any change and the history of the Bible shows its accuracy.

Claim of Jesus

After establishing on independent grounds that the Bible is historically trustworthy, we then go to the Bible to see what it says. The main character is Jesus Christ. Jesus claimed to be the unique Son of God. There is no denying that Jesus made these claims.

Resurrection

Merely making these claims, however, does not prove them to be true. The Bible says Jesus demonstrated Himself to be the Son of God by His resurrection from the dead (Romans 1:4). The evidence that Jesus came back from the dead is more than sufficient to any person wishing to know the truth of the matter.

Testimony of Jesus

Because Jesus demonstrated Himself to be God in human flesh, He speaks with ultimate authority on every matter. Whatever He says concerning any issue is the final word. Jesus made it clear that the Old Testament was God's Word. He also pre-authenticated the New Testament in granting the gift of "total recall" to His disciples.

Therefore, based upon the testimony of Jesus, the church maintains that the Bible is the infallible Word of God. This line of reasoning is not arguing in a circle but rather drawing logical conclusions from the facts.

Taste and See

We have seen that there is sufficient reason to believe that God has revealed Himself to mankind and that this revelation is recorded in Scripture. Once a person sees that the evidence for belief in the God of the Bible is sufficient, he or she must make the final step, an act of faith. The Bible encourages the individual to personally test the claims of God. The psalmist wrote: "Oh, taste and see that the Lord is good" (Psalm 34:8).

The offer that Jesus made to the people of His day is still valid today,

> Come to Me, all you who labor and are heavy laden, and I will give you rest. Take My yoke upon you and learn from Me, for I am gentle and lowly in heart, and you will find rest for your souls (Matthew 11:28, 29).

ABOUT THE AUTHOR

Don Stewart

Don Stewart is one of the most successful writers in the country having authored or co-authored over twenty books. These include *You Be The Judge, The Coming Temple* and *Ten Reasons To Trust the Bible.*

Don's writings have also achieved international success. Twenty-four of his titles have been translated into different languages including Chinese, Finnish, Polish, Spanish, German, and Portuguese.

Don received his undergraduate degree at Biola University majoring in Bible. He received a masters degree from Talbot Theological Seminary graduating with the highest honors. Don is a member of the national honor society, Kappa Tau Epsilon.

Don is also an internationally known apologist, a defender of the historic Christian faith. In his defense of Christianity he has traveled to over thirty countries speaking at colleges, universities, churches, seminars, and retreats. His topics include the evidence for Christianity, the identity of Jesus Christ, the challenge of the cults, and the relationship of the Bible and science.

Because of his international success as an author and speaker, Don's various books have generated sales of over one million copies.

Other Books By Don Stewart from Dart Press

You Be The Judge: Is Christianity True?

Ten Reasons To Trust The Bible (formerly titled The Ten Wonders Of The Bible).

The Coming Temple (with Chuck Missler)

Basic Bible Study Series

* What Everyone Needs To Know About **God**
* What Everyone Needs To Know About **Jesus**
* What Everyone Needs To Know About **The Holy Spirit**

To order books call toll free 1-800-637-5177

Books Coming From Don Stewart in 1992

In Search of the Lost Ark: The Quest for the Ark of the Covenant

Basic Bible Study Series

* What The Bible Says About **Science**
* What The Bible Says About **The Future**